P9-ARC-427

THE WINE REGION OF
RIOJA

THE WINE REGION OF
RIOJA

ANA FABIANO

STERLING EPICURE
New York

STERLING EPICURE
New York

An Imprint of Sterling Publishing
387 Park Avenue South
New York, NY 10016

STERLING EPICURE is a trademark of Sterling Publishing Co., Inc. The distinctive Sterling logo
is a registered trademark of Sterling Publishing Co., Inc.

© 2012 by Ana Fabiano
Maps © 2012 by Jeffrey L. Ward

All rights reserved. No part of this publication may be reproduced,
stored in a retrieval system, or transmitted, in any form or by any means,
electronic, mechanical, photocopying, recording, or otherwise,
without prior written permission from the publisher.

ISBN 978-1-4027-5403-6 (hardcover)

Distributed in Canada by Sterling Publishing
^c/o Canadian Manda Group, 165 Dufferin Street
Toronto, Ontario, Canada M6K 3H6
Distributed in the United Kingdom by GMC Distribution Services
Castle Place, 166 High Street, Lewes, East Sussex, England BN7 1XU
Distributed in Australia by Capricorn Link (Australia) Pty. Ltd.
P.O. Box 704, Windsor, NSW 2756, Australia

Designed by Christine Heun

For information about custom editions, special sales, and premium and corporate purchases,
please contact Sterling Special Sales at 800-805-5489 or specialsales@sterlingpublishing.com.

Manufactured in China

2 4 6 8 10 9 7 5 3 1

www.sterlingpublishing.com

BOOK OPENER: **The Berceo Valley**
PREVIOUS PAGES: **The Ebro River**
OPPOSITE: **Enological Station of Haro**

for the people and
wine professionals of
RIOJA

PREFACE

Every circuitous journey has a first step, and my thirty-year relationship with Spain, and especially with Rioja, is no exception. It began in a classroom at Douglass College, the women's college of Rutgers University in New Jersey. The person I credit with the course my life has taken is Dr. Micaela Misiego.

Dr. Misiego was chairperson of the Romance language department, had high standards, and encouraged her students to perfect their language skills by studying in Europe. During lectures she sometimes would drift off into stories of the Spanish Civil War from her memories as a young girl in Catalonia, leaning on her desk for emotional support. I followed her directive and headed to Madrid for my junior year abroad.

The Spain I found in 1980, however, was not the same as the one from which Dr. Misiego had fled. The years from 1978 to 1982 have been called Spain's Transition to Democracy, and it was a captivating time to be in the country. After forty-three years of fear, suffering, and suffocation, the energy of the country was unleashed and rules could be broken just for the fun of it.

These were historic years around the world, and I spent them with my Madrileño friends talking politics all night, with Bruce Springsteen, Bob Marley, Peter Gabriel, Mecano, and Miguel Rios blasting in the background. It was a time of unrest. John Lennon had been murdered, and there had been attempts on the lives of both President Ronald Reagan and Pope John Paul XXIII. In Spain there was an attempted coup against the new democracy on February 23, 1981; Antonio Tejero led it, and members of the legislature were held hostage. It was a tumultuous time to be a student there and exhilarating to be in a country that was launching its constitution.

After completing a graduate program in Madrid I returned to New York and became the first American to be hired by the Embassy of Spain's trade office. Spain had begun to privatize its industry and establish export associations, and the wine industry was a targeted sector. I served as a founding member of the Wines from Spain center when there were only three main *Denominación de Origen* (DO) regions: Cava for sparking wine, Jerez for its legendary sherry, and Rioja for fine wines. At that time there were just eighteen Rioja bodegas exporting wine to the United States and fewer than eighty registered in the whole DO region.

My first trip to Rioja was in 1987 as chaperone for a group of journalists, and I vividly recall the region's beauty and the generosity of its people, experiences I have had countless times on subsequent trips. I also recall the lively discussions with legendary winemakers as well as wonderful meals with special cellar picks of Gran Reservas.

Now, more than twenty-five years after the transition to democracy officially ended, I remain mesmerized by how the country has emerged from its prison cell into stardom. As Spain reaches new heights, Rioja is on a parallel track. Now sitting alongside the historic Reserva and Gran Reserva wines still blended and aged according to a rich tradition, there are incredible wines made from 100 percent Tempranillo or Graciano and there are Tempranillo Blanco wines, too. From 18 bodegas exporting wine to the United States in the 1980s, there are now more than 170. From fewer than one hundred bodegas, there are now six hundred registered in the *Denominación de Origen Calificada* (DOCa).

Rioja has emerged to take its rightful place among a small group of great red wine regions of the world. Despite this well-deserved achievement, there are few books in English on Rioja. Most wine books include a page or a

small section, inadequate even to skim the surface of the region and its wines.

In 2007 I studied and sat for the Instituto Cervantes examination, the most rigorous given by the Spanish Ministry of Education. When I received my mastery certification, I felt ready for this work.

I delved into all types of Castilian books, which you will find listed in the bibliography, and conducted numerous interviews with revered and encyclopedic Riojans who have studied their region and the growth of its wine industry but do not speak English. The knowledge conveyed in this book also encompasses more than twenty years of journal notes from many trips; it includes conversations with two and three generations of winemakers and more than twenty-five years of tasting Riojan wines.

But wine is not the only aspect of Rioja to explore, and my research took me deep into the history of the region and its language to discover its unique spirit, which is so inviting to visitors today. On my last research trip for this book, I packed up my seventeen-year-old son and headed to Haro for the annual pilgrimage of San Felices and the Battle of Wine.

A few months earlier, a very kind winemaker friend had given me the inside scoop on the day's events and how to prepare for them. Early in the morning, we journeyed by foot the 4 miles (6 kilometers) to Bilibio to see the tiny chapel where a mass would begin the saints day homage. I felt comforted at this luminous place where I experienced peace, love, and faith. The sermon centered on the celebration of saints and the tremendous joy and blessing that adventure brings to our lives.

Little did we know that adventure was awaiting us as soon as we left the church. The Battle of Wine folk were lying in wait to blast the churchgoers on their steep descent down the mountain. There they were, armed with red grape must and pressure tanks. We all walked arm in arm a few hundred feet and then found a corner spot to prepare a lunch of warm chorizo, fresh bread, and luscious Reservas and listen to a band of trumpeters.

That afternoon we squirted and were doused in return. We ran and we hid, and we laughed out loud. At one point my son, Nick, and I gazed at hillsides full of purple figures. I said that it was like Woodstock, and he replied that it was a lot more. After complete head-to-toe saturation we all paraded back to Haro, soaked in happiness, adventure, and tannins.

I hope this will be the first of many books dedicated to the region of Rioja. It is truly an honor for me to be a voice for this ancient land, its people, its wines, and its singular spirit.

Ana Fabiano
New York, New York

OPPOSITE: The Vineyards of Bodegas Muga
FOLLOWING PAGES: Poppy Field and Vineyard in Tricio

La Rioja:
A Magical Place

1

Rioja is beautiful. I find it simply breathtaking —a viewpoint that has been validated by a wide array of wine journalists, chefs, wine connoisseurs, gourmands, and family members. Rioja is worth the journey.

The best analogy may be that La Rioja is like a mixed salad with the best of everything in it. Its ingredients include superlative climate, soil, products, vineyards, gardens, orchards, people, history, culture, agriculture, spirit, beauty, and tradition. Then they are dressed with a combination of beauty, calm, peace, and harmony. Contentment reigns there.

It is important to know that Rioja is one name for two different geographic areas. One is La Rioja the political region, which has a boundary different from that of the second, Rioja the wine region. The wine region expands out of La Rioja and into Álava in the Basque Country in the northwest and Navarre in the northeast. Within the wine region of Rioja there are three subregions—Rioja Alta, Rioja Alavesa, and Rioja Baja— each with its own geography and characteristics. But all these overlapping regions and subregions are united by the terrain—the rivers, valleys, and mountains that form this place. The Rioja wine region will be discussed specifically in Chapter 3, where you will find descriptions of all of the important elements—natural, historical, and human—that have created such a magical place.

THE ALL-IMPORTANT EBRO RIVER

"If there's a river in your upbringing, you'll probably always hear it."

This anonymous line could have been penned for the Ebro as it meanders through La Rioja. The Ebro River and the mountain ranges on either side of it form the yin and yang of La Rioja, as the juxtaposition of rivers and mountains does all over the world. Residents of the land, regardless of whether they live in the heights of the mountains or on the gentle banks of the river, have a relationship with both.

The Ebro is positioned like the spinal cord that runs down the center of this fertile region. The river, which is 566 miles (911 kilometers) in length, is the longest in Spain. Its source is aptly named Pico de los Tres Mares (Peak of the Three Seas) and is in Cantabria, from which it flows to the east and empties into the warm waters of the Mediterranean Sea just below Barcelona, in the region of Catalonia. As it travels, it creates the Ebro Depression, which separates the Pyrenees Mountains from the Sistema Ibérico, an interlocking series of mountain ranges. From the air La Rioja looks like a large bowl; it is a depression created by the Ebro and flanked on three sides by mountains.

The Ebro receives water from more than two hundred tributaries. Those on the left bank (to the north of the river), which originate in the rainy Pyrenees, contribute the overwhelming majority of its water; the right-bank tributaries, such as most of those in La Rioja, are much smaller.

The importance of the Ebro is reflected in the name of the Iberian Peninsula itself. The river was known as the Iber or Iberus before it was the Ebro. A Greek writer in the sixth century BCE wrote about the Iberians, the people who lived along the Iber River.

Rivers play the role of protagonist in their regions, and the Ebro is no exception. In 1521, the walled area of the city of Logroño, which now is the city's Old Quarter (Casco Antiguo), was under attack by the French army of Francis I, led by Count André de Foix. The Logroñese heroically resisted the attack, which lasted for two weeks. They fought starvation by sneaking out at night through their *calados*—the underground tunnels that connected family cellars—down to the Ebro, where they fished and brought their catch back to their homes. With wine from their cellars, fish, and bread, they survived until the troops of King Charles I, led by the Duke of Nájera, came to their rescue.

The victory occurred on June 11, and the next day was traditionally the Feast of San Bernabé, which the city now celebrates as a local holiday. To remember this great event, thousands of people come together every year at the remains of the city wall, El Revellín, and get a portion of fish, bread, and wine from the Brotherhood of the Fish (*Cofradía del Pez*), which oversees the proceedings.

THE SEVEN VALLEYS

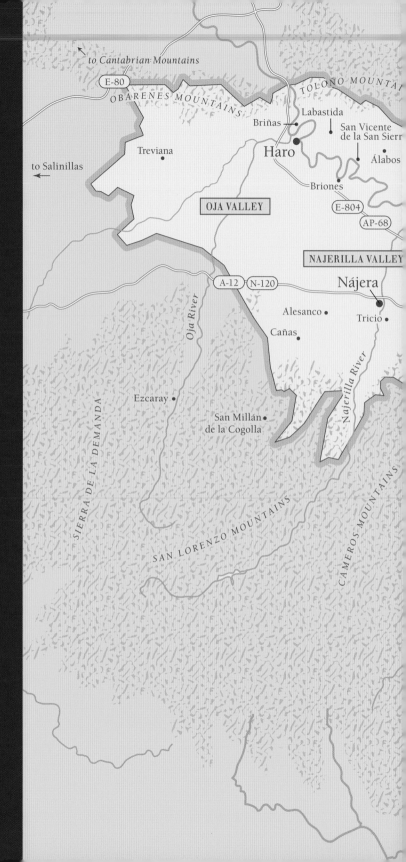

The importance of The Ebro in La Rioja extends beyond its own banks. Feeding into the Ebro on its right bank, flowing from south to north, are seven small yet significant tributaries that form seven valleys. With the change of climate over the centuries these rivers today are like gentle streams as they join the Ebro on its flow to the Mediterranean.

These tributaries irrigate the vineyards and orchards, and each valley contains more small valleys in which the rich land is cultivated. In fact, in the valleys of La Rioja formed by these tributaries one can find 36 percent of the biodiversity in all of Spain; this kind of richness is found in only 1 percent of the country's regions.

In addition to flora and fauna, the valleys offer a panoply of landscapes, all within a few miles of one another. There are striking rock formations with soil the color of rich ocher, canyons dotted with majestic evergreens, peaks jutting out from seemingly barren land, and mountain zones too high to support crops.

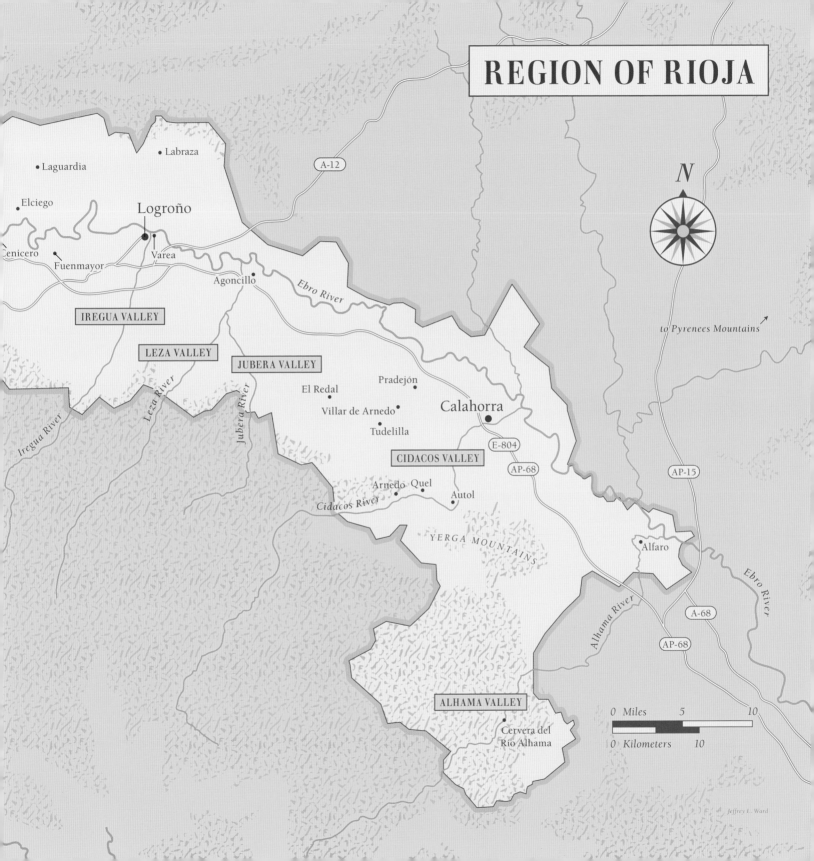

REGION OF RIOJA

Laguardia

Labraza

Elciego

Logroño

Cenicero

Varea

Fuenmayor

Agoncillo

A-12

Ebro River

IREGUA VALLEY

LEZA VALLEY

JUBERA VALLEY

Leza River

Jubera River

Iregua River

El Redal

Pradejón

Villar de Arnedo

Calahorra

Tudelilla

CIDACOS VALLEY

E-804

AP-68

Arnedo Quel

Autol

Cidacos River

YERGA MOUNTAINS

Alfaro

to Pyrenees Mountains

AP-15

Ebro River

Alhama River

A-68

AP-68

ALHAMA VALLEY

Cervera del
Río Alhama

N

0 Miles 5 10

0 Kilometers 10

Jeffrey L. Ward

OJA VALLEY

The Oja River flows into the Ebro in the small city of Haro near the western border of Rioja. In and to the northwest of this valley are many of the "Alta Alta" vineyard villages—the highest and most remote and also some of the highest in quality of the Rioja Alta subregion. The Oja Valley is also influenced by the Sierra de la Demanda range, which has the longest-lasting snowcaps among the mountains on the right bank. The range adds volume to the valley's rivers long into the spring.

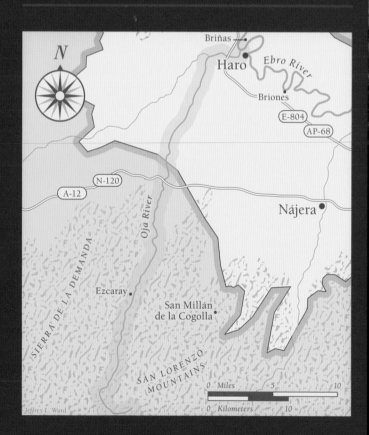

NAJERILLA VALLEY

East of the Oja, this valley has the greatest concentration of vines in Rioja, as well as many other Riojan riches. The high slopes of the Sierra de la Demanda and the cold waters of the Najerilla River create fabled beauty throughout the region. Terraces and slopes of vines run parallel to the river in many areas, and forests of beech and oak trees are interspersed with the vineyards. Every small valley in the Najerilla Valley seems more beautiful than the next.

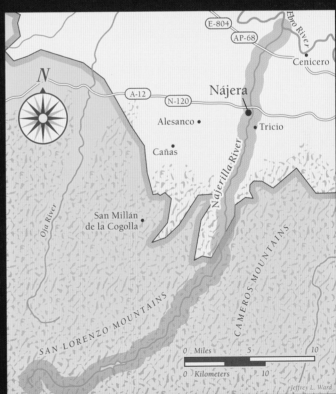

IREGUA VALLEY

The Iregua Valley forms the dividing line between the Rioja Alta and Rioja Baja subregions; many Riojans refer to it as Rioja Media. After passing through the valley, the Iregua flows directly into Logroño, the capital of La Rioja. On the right bank of the Ebro, minutes from Logroño, is the village of Varea, known for its produce gardens and orchards. Iregua Valley views include groves of olive trees and other crops as well as vineyards.

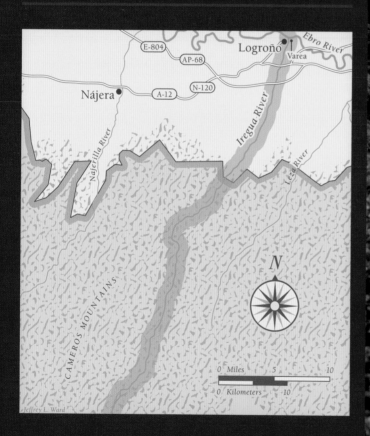

LEZA VALLEY

The Leza River joins the Jubera River before emptying into the Ebro. The Leza Valley forms a dividing point between the greener, fertile mountain ranges to the south and west and the drier, more arid mountain ranges to the east. Striking canyons in the Leza Valley make it easily identifiable from afar.

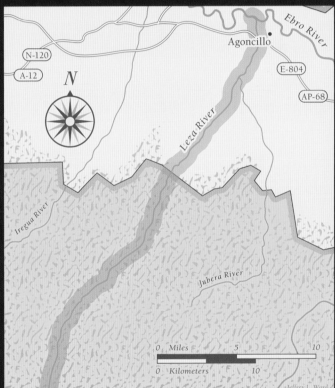

JUBERA VALLEY

The Jubera River is the shortest of the Ebro's tributaries in La Rioja; it is a mere 25 miles (40 kilometers) in length. The palette of the mountains surrounding this valley is marked with sienna and other earth tones, and Jubera Valley is home to noted wine villages such as Murillo de Rio Leza, Ventas Blancas, Santa Engracia del Jubera, and Robres del Castillo.

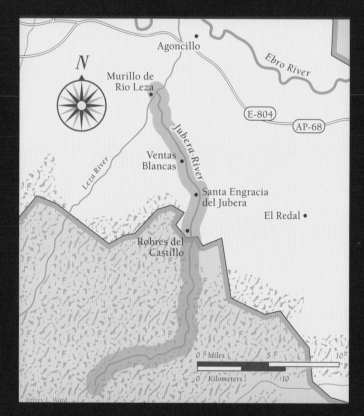

CIDACOS VALLEY

Situated in the Rioja Baja subregion, the little Cidacos River, which lacks the volume of the Najerilla or the Iregua, snakes through the valley and passes by the town of Calahorra on its way to the Ebro. The Cidacos Valley has a far more Mediterranean climate than the neighboring areas, and these fertile lowlands produce a cornucopia of fruit and vegetable crops. It is only at the higher elevations, in villages such as Arnedo, Quel, and Autol, that the abundant small parcels of land are filled by vineyards.

ALHAMA VALLEY

The arid slopes and hills of the alhama valley are subject to Mediterranean heat, so the vineyards occupy the higher elevations and the lowlands host groves of olive, fruit, and almond trees as well as vegetable farms. It is in this warm valley that the Rioja grape harvest begins each year. The valley is bordered by the majestic Yerga Mountains, which contain numerous hermit caves from centuries past as well as vast and spacious vineyards.

THE ROLE OF THE MOUNTAINS

Spain is said to be surpassed only by Switzerland for the title of Europe's most mountainous country, and its mountain ranges play a significant role in the country's climate, geopolitical history, and economy. This is clearly true in Rioja, which is dominated by more than 150 square miles (40,000 hectares) of interlocking mountain ranges.

In Rioja the mountains are not just a geographic demarcation—they are protective. Their height allows them to shield the land from both cold and warm winds. For example, the Cantabrian Mountains are credited with shielding the Alavesa and Rioja Alta subregions from the strong, cold Atlantic winds; the Sierra de la Demanda blocks the western winds; and the Yerga Mountains of the Rioja Baja shield the vineyards from whistling, warm Mediterranean gusts from the east.

Rioja's mountains define it as a region. Riojans often refer to the Valley Zone, known for its treasured vines, and the Mountain Zone, with its abundance of forests. Even those in the mountain villages view their region's Valley Zone with great reverence and pride.

RIGHT: Mount San Lorenzo and the Najerilla Valley

THE INTRICATE HISTORY OF A RICH LAND

For a region of such tranquility and beauty, the history of La Rioja is one characterized by centuries of conflict. When the Romans arrived in the second century BCE, they found the area inhabited by three tribes of Celtic origin. The Vascones, an ancient people who are most likely the ancestors of the present-day Basques (and from whom the name *Basque* is derived), were the dominant group; the other peoples populating the region were the Berones and the Autrigones.

The Romans considered the area part of Hispania Tarraconensis, the northeasternmost province of Hispania, and artifacts from Roman times can be found throughout La Rioja. Although the fields have been tilled for many centuries, farmers continue to discover tools, coins, and pieces of glassware and mosaics in the soil.

By 476 CE the Roman Empire had collapsed, and Visigoth tribes invaded from the north, to be replaced in 711 by the Moors, who invaded from the south and ruled much of Spain for more than seven hundred years; during this time La Rioja was part of the region called Al Andalus. The centuries that followed were characterized by countless small wars during which the incipient Christian kingdoms tried to regain dominance of the region. In the early tenth century, Sancho I of Pamplona conquered most of the area, and La Rioja formed the independent Kingdom of Viguera from 970 to 1005.

After the independence of Castile in 1035, there were constant border disputes between Castile and Navarre to gain control of La Rioja until arbitration was sought from King Henry I of England. In 1177 he decided in favor of Castile, but the disputes over who owned this verdant region continued. In 1369 Aragon and Navarre signed a pact that transferred La Rioja to Aragon, but it was soon recovered by Castile.

The decision of the Constitutional Cortes (effectively Spain's first constitution) declared La Rioja an independent province in 1812, and this was followed ten years later in 1822 by the creation of the province of Logroño. However, King Ferdinand VII annulled those decisions soon afterward. The provinces of Burgos, Soria, Álava, Navarre, and Aragon once again divided up the historic villages of La Rioja. In 1833 a royal decree created the approximate boundaries of the region we know today, which became a provincial autonomous community in 1982.

THE IMPORTANCE OF THE PILGRIMAGE ROUTE

The walking route to pay homage of the remains of Saint James (Santiago in Spanish), the martyred Apostle of Christ, has been used by European pilgrims for more than a millennium. Logroño became an official stop on the pilgrimage routes in the early ninth century, and the route itself, most of which goes north of La Rioja, has played a significant role in the region's history.

27

The Camino de Santiago (the Way of Saint James) is not a single route; it is a large network of ancient pilgrim routes stretching across Europe that converge at the tomb of Santiago de Compostela in northwestern Spain. The Camino Francés (the French route), for example, is almost 500 miles (780 kilometers) in length and begins at a village near Biarritz; some of the smaller routes from other nations intersect with it in Logroño.

Saint James is important to Christians as one of the twelve Apostles of Christ. During his life, he spread the gospel in the northwestern part of Spain. On a return trip to Palestine in 44 CE, he was captured and beheaded by Herod Agrippa. His followers stole his body and transported it by boat to a hiding place on the west coast of Spain. In 813 a hermit found his remains, and the church of Santiago de Compostela was constructed on the site. The scallop shell has become the symbol of Santiago and the pilgrimage routes. One reason for this may be the legend that the body of Santiago was lost in a storm off the Spanish coast yet washed ashore undamaged, covered in scallop shells. But the scallop shell also serves as a metaphor for the pilgrimage routes. Just as the grooves in the shell converge on a single point, so the many pilgrimage routes all end at Santiago de Compostela.

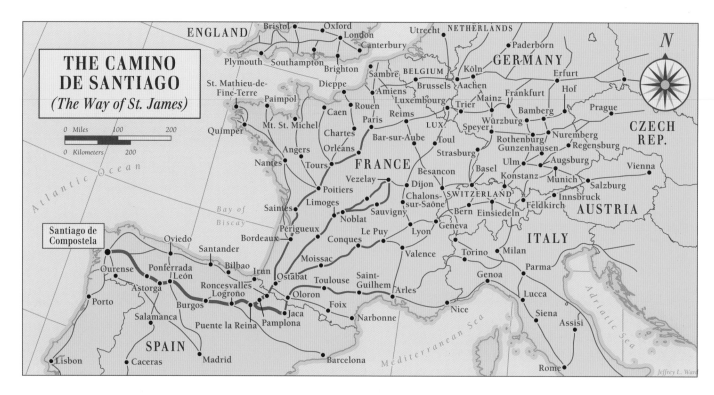

LOGROÑO'S KEEPER OF THE CAMINO DE SANTIAGO

Although Logroño is connected to the rest of Spain by major highways, the Camino de Santiago remains a one-lane dirt road as it passes through the capital of La Rioja. Luca, a strapping twenty-one-year-old Milanese man, and Woonsook, a petite thirty-seven-year old Korean woman were just two of the visitors on a bright September morning to have their pilgrimage passports stamped by María Teodora Mediavilla, now seventy-six, and her daughter, Felisa, now forty-six.

Since the family moved to Logroño in 1940, three generations of women have greeted pilgrims at this site under a spreading fig tree that produces a bounty of fruit as well as shade. María's mother, who had been recruited to the work by a parish priest, died in 1982, and María took over from her. The women sell soft drinks and some scallop-shaped souvenirs but give away everything else. By 6 a.m. each day they are making coffee and baking bread to nourish both bodies and souls.

María says she is "half house mother and half psychiatrist" to those who pass through her stop on their monthlong walk. If the weather is unusually bad, she allows them to sleep overnight on the first floor of her house, and many of them confide in her about the inner demons that led them to the pilgrimage. And there are many stories to tell. An average month sees 350 visitors, but in the prime months of May and September the number can be double or triple that.

María and Felisa have a collection of twenty-seven leatherbound books containing written comments from pilgrims going back to 1960. And all those thousands of pilgrims have an oval stamp on their pilgrimage passport with the words *Camino de Santiago* and *Logroño* on the outer edge. Inside the oval is *Felisa*, the name of the family's house, with the words *Higos, Agua y Amor* (*figs, water and love*) beneath.

THE HISTORY OF THE JEWISH COMMUNITY IN LA RIOJA

Spain had a flourishing Jewish community for fifteen centuries until the monarchs Ferdinand and Isabella signed the Edict of Expulsion on March 31, 1492. The prominence of Jews in Spanish society over a period of about three hundred years known as the Golden Age coincided with the centuries of Moorish rule, which lasted from the conquest in 711 CE to the end of the eleventh century. Hispanic Jews were active in all levels of Spanish society, ranging from great *cortesanos* (courtiers) and financiers to artists, small merchants, and farmers. In La Rioja there are records of relatively large Jewish populations in Haro, Nájera, and Calahorra.

During the reconquest of Spain by the Christians, the presence and contributions of the Jewish community as an ally were vital to the repopulation and regional reorganization. Many Jews spoke Arabic, and this linguistic advantage made their role important in several capacities, including diplomatic negotiations with the Moors.

Although they were integrated into Spanish society in some respects during this time, the Jews maintained separate communities with their own judicial, religious, and gastronomic traditions. Councils of Spanish officials and Jewish representatives were held to establish a just rate of taxation for Jewish communities and devise an equitable system for the collection of taxes. The bishops of various districts assumed authority over the Jews and in conjunction with Jewish representatives formed rules to govern the communities, including the regular election of rabbis and judges.

Evidently the Jewish community enjoyed wine; it was as important in Jewish tradition as it was in Spanish culture. "Wine is a symbol of happiness and that is why it is blessed at parties and important Jewish ceremonies," said the author and scholar Uriel Macías, who organized a conference on the role of wine in Jewish culture at the Vivanco Museum in Briones in 2006.

Records show active Jewish participation in and ownership of vineyards in the region's three principal monasteries of San Millán, Santa María la Real, and La Valvanera beginning in the eleventh century. Well into the thirteenth and fourteenth centuries vineyard sales and exchange records prove the ownership by Jews of parcels in the river basins of the Tirón, Najerilla, Iregua, and Cicados as well as Jews' compulsory contributions to the mother monasteries and churches. These deeds, however, are all that remain because all vestiges of Jewish culture were obliterated after the expulsion or forced conversion of the Jews in 1492.

THE ROLE OF THE WOOL INDUSTRY

Spain secured a prominent position in the world wool industry as early as 1000 CE, having bred the merino sheep with its particularly fine wool. Spain's vast mountain terrain provided the perfect topography for profitable sheep herding, especially in northern regions such as

Rioja where fertile green pastures were abundant. Another major grazing land was in the Soria region, to the south of Rioja Baja, which Castile acquired in the tenth century. This eased the grazing pressure on lands in Rioja that were intended to be used as vineyard land.

In 1273, the Mesta, a powerful association of sheep owners, was formed to protect the lucrative interests of the merino industry. Under its control, legal right of way was created for the migration of flocks to different grazing lands in the spring and fall. One of those routes extended from the Mountain Zone village of Ezcaray all the way to Extremadura in central western Spain; another moved the animals from the Cameros Mountains of

La Rioja to Andalucía in the far south, about 400 miles (635 kilometers). These routes were established long before the current vineyards, and over the centuries shepherds preserved their ancestral right to pass over lands regardless of the crops being cultivated.

"Sheep migration was customary and a significant part of the scenery and livelihood in Rioja until the eighteenth century," says Luis Elías Pastor, a Riojan historian and scholar. He points out that the wool from free-roaming sheep was considered to be of much higher quality than that from fenced animals. Once the sheep were enclosed, they were used only for meat rather than being shorn for cloth production.

In the sixteenth century, Spain guaranteed its dominance of the wool industry by outlawing the export of merino sheep except by royal permission. This created a strong monopoly on the breed. Suddenly, Spanish exports of woolen fabrics became more than ten times greater than those from England, a leading exporter of wool to other European countries.

This early lucrative wool industry was controlled predominantly by the *conversos*, Jews who remained in Spain and converted to Christianity after the Edict of Expulsion of 1492. All the royal textile factories and workrooms were centered in La Rioja, and much of the money the *conversos* made from the wool trade was reinvested in wineries. For hundreds of years in Spain, the wool industry was of central importance, and without it winemaking would not have the history in Rioja that it does.

Wool and mohair are still woven in Ezcaray, located in the Mountain Zone high above the Oja Valley. Natural dyes are used whose formulation dates back centuries. However, the rise of synthetic materials in the twentieth century diminished the importance of wool, as it did in all wool-producing countries around the world.

THE CREATION OF THE CASTILIAN LANGUAGE

Spanish today—also known by the name of the primary dialect in Spain, Castilian—is the native language of half a billion people in twenty countries; it is even the official language at the Argentinean and Chilean outposts in Antarctica. It is second only to Mandarin Chinese in its number of native speakers, and it is one of the five official languages of the United Nations. It all began at the Yuso monastery in La Rioja.

Spanish evolved from the Latin introduced to the Iberian Peninsula by the Romans during the Second Punic War in the third century BCE. Over hundreds of years, local pronunciations and usage developed independently in different regions, including the central region of Castile. The earliest written materials to use Castilian, in the form of notes on Latin texts—referred to as "glosses," from which we get our word *glossary*—date from the mid-eleventh century, and works of literature in Castilian Spanish first appeared in the mid-twelfth century. The most important of these glosses is the *Glosas Emilianenses*, kept at the Yuso monastery library, which appears to have words of both Castilian and Basque in its margins. Monasteries in nearby Burgos also contain examples of these writings.

As the Christian reconquest of Spain from the Moors progressed southward, Castilian moved with it. It was in Madrid and Toledo by the eleventh century, and in the thirteenth century King Alfonso X, who was called the Learned King, fostered its progress. Working from his court in Toledo, scholars wrote original works in Castilian and translated everything from histories to literary works into Castilian from other languages, primarily Latin.

The importance of the Yuso monastery as the birthplace of modern Spanish was reinforced in the thirteenth century. Gonzalo de Berceo was educated and lived at the Yuso monastery. This medieval writer and poet's compositions raised Castilian to the status of a literary language.

In the late fifteenth century when the regions of Castile and León merged with Aragón, Castilian became the official language of Spain for written and educational purposes, although several spoken dialects remained, especially in the southern region of Andalucía. Antonio de Nebrija's *Gramática de la lengua castellana* (*Grammar of the Castilian Language*) was written in 1492 and became the handbook for Castilian as it was exported to Spanish colonies worldwide.

OPPOSITE: Sheep in the Leza Valley
RIGHT: *Glosas Emilianenses*

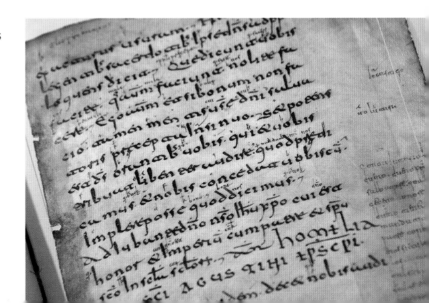

HOW RIOJA WAS NAMED

There are twenty-two theories about the origin of the name of this ancient wine region, but only two of them are considered credible by respected regional scholars because they have both phonetic and etymological arguments to support them. Both of these theories refer to the landscape.

The first, which is drawn from Latin sources, is that the name *Rioja* derives from *Rialia*, a word that refers to the collection of small tributaries in the region, which created a small triangular territory that corresponds to part of the Oja Valley of today's Rioja Alta and the Mountain Zone near Ezcaray. In Latin the final letter *a* was neutral and plural; thus, the word referred to a collection of rivers. Over the centuries it evolved from *Rialia* to *Riolia*, and from the Latin *li* to the Castilian *ll*, hence *Riolla* and finally *Rioja*.

In the tenth century, the term *Rialia* was clearly referenced in Codex 31, housed in the library at the Yuso monastery in San Millán, and thereafter many times again in subsequent codices. It also is included in written correspondence that remains in libraries throughout Spain.

The second theory is derived from Euskara, the language of the Basque Country, which is considered by most scholars to be the oldest known language still in existence; there is evidence that it was spoken in the Upper Paleolithic Era about 25,000 years ago. It is known that by the ninth century there was a significant Basque population in the Rioja Valley, so the language was widely spoken.

The archives in the Yuso monastery document the inclusion of Basque words alongside those in Old Castilian. Old Basque maps called today's Rioja *Arrioixa*, which means "land of rocks." From there it evolved into *Rioxa*. With the growth of Castilian, the letter *x* was converted to a *j*, and the word evolved into *Rioja*.

At the same time there is evidence that the monks at the Suso and Yuso monasteries were of both local and Basque origin. It seems logical that both developments of the word *Rioja* evolved together just as those people lived alongside one another.

LA RIOJA'S MAJOR TOWNS

Because of La Rioja's small size, its major towns are so close to one another that visitors to the region can explore them all in a few days. Riojans are much more comfortable in the role of host than that of guest. Because the region was a passageway for so many centuries, Riojans historically have entertained pilgrims and enophiles alike.

LOGROÑO

The capital of La Rioja and centrally located within the three wine subregions, Logroño, on the banks of the Ebro, was pulled back into the fold of Christian Spain when that grand hero of Spain's reconquest, El Cid, conquered the city in 1092.

Half of La Rioja's population of 300,000 lives in Logroño, and about 20 percent of the citizens are involved in the wine trade, as they have been for centuries. Documents in Logroño's city hall dating from 1095 show that there were mandates for vineyard care, and a city ordinance, dated 1595, prohibited the passage of carriages on Ruavieja Street for fear that the vibration caused by the traffic would affect the wines aging in subterranean cellars. By the end of the seventeenth century the cellars under Logroño would store more than 6 million liters of wine, roughly 375,000 cases.

Visitors to Logroño find that this small city maintains an unspoiled innocence. The Old Quarter, the Casco Antiguo, is considered the most enchanting part of the city and has many pedestrian streets filled with tapas bars, restaurants, shops, and monuments. Calle Laurel, along with adjacent streets such as Calle San Juan, forms a small matrix of alleyways full of big flavors from tapas paired with glasses of wine. For a list of tapas bars, see page 37.

Visitors will not find streets lined with shops bearing the names Prada, Armani, and Starbucks. Logroño is truly a city of Old World charm, the type that is increasingly difficult to find. It is still easy to encounter Logroñese who do not speak English but will wholeheartedly manage to give you directions or escort you to where you need to go. Small shopkeepers still provide service with pride and personal care in the same way that vintners create wine.

There is an air of contentment in Logroño. Residents live comfortably in a place they often describe as a "city to live in." Distances are short and lend themselves to maintaining friendships and family life with ease. The city is filled with beautiful architecture that has been restored sensitively.

RIGHT: Subterranean Wine Cellar in Logroño

A TAPAS CRAWL IN LOGROÑO

Regardless of the regionalism that characterizes Spain, the country is united by the Spaniards' need to socialize. A Spaniard would prefer one more hour of conversation to an extra hour of sleep. The tapas culture is an outgrowth of this spirit; it originated in Spain but has crossed many culinary borders. The cultural importance of food and wine in Spain is integral to the social experience and permeates every region, including Rioja.

No trip to Logroño is complete without the experience of nibbling one's way through at least some of the fifty-plus *taperías* on the narrow pedestrian streets in the Old Quarter. Here one will find multiple generations of Riojans commingling, as well as national and international visitors enjoying a vital aspect of life in Logroño.

Calle Laurel (Laurel Street), pronounced **ki**-yay laur-**el**, is the epicenter for a tapas trek, together with a few even smaller and narrower streets adjacent to it, Calle San Juan and Calle San Agustín. These tapas bars began more than a century ago, and it is not just their food that makes them so special; it is also the scene.

On any weekend night every bar is as crowded as a New York City subway platform at rush hour. Once you elbow your way in, the way to get a glass of red wine is to yell *"Un Rioja!"* at the barman; in this part of the world the name says it all. If the bar person hears you, you continue the task of moving past the three or four people ahead of you to order your tapas.

You have only one glass of wine (which is usually less than $2) and one tapa (never more than $5) per spot because there are so many places awaiting you. So with a glass in one hand and a small plate in the other, it is time to retreat to one of the tables placed around the bar, from which people watching has been elevated almost to an art form.

With all these taperías side by side, you would think that there would be cutthroat competition, but Logroño and its barkeepers are extremely civilized. The reason you do not see any "two for one" signs is that each spot has a specific dish for which it is known. If you are not aware of the dish, just look around when you walk in. Chances are, you will see the same food on almost all plates, and it is a good idea to order the same thing.

After many trips, one comes to know the favorites. Here they are:

- **ELECTRA RIOJA GRAN CASINO**. The architecture is postmodern, and the dish to try is *bacalao* with black olive tapenade; the salt cod is cooked so well that it almost tastes fresh.

- **JUAN Y JUAN**. This is a new addition to the circuit, and it specializes in traditional fire-roasted baby lamb chops and also a goat cheese dish served with marmalade.

- **LA GOTA DE VINO**. This bar is known for *bocadillos*, which are little bites of many foods on one plate.

- **LA TASCA DEL PATO**. Try the grilled white asparagus coated with local Camerano cheese and the fish cakes.

- **LAS CUBANAS**. Roast suckling pig is a delicacy in Rioja, and this bar is the place to sample it.

- **LAS QUEJAS**. This is a nice place to start a crawl: The ham and cheese sandwiches are not to be missed, and the environment is warm and inviting.

- **BAR LORENZO**. The dish to order here is skewers of chorizo sausage and grilled lamb in a spicy and sweet sauce

- **LOS ROTOS**. Spain is famous for its egg sandwiches, and this is a place to try one, but equally delicious is a small grilled steak served with a berry relish and a dried fruit compote.

- **PATA NEGRA**. Situated on a corner, this bar is named for Spain's famous black-hoofed pigs and has a mural of pigs across one wall. The dish to try is a sandwich of Serrano ham, tomato, and anchovy.

- **BAR SEBAS**. Although this landmark is known for its Spanish *tortilla*, a potato omelet, it also offers a piquillo pepper stuffed with ground meat in a creamy béchamel sauce.

- **BAR SORIANO**. The sign for this bar, a landmark on the circuit, is a retro mushroom, and with good reason. It specializes in wild mushrooms cooked with garlic and served with an optional shrimp on a skewer.

- **TESTAVÍN**. This is a hip place with modern tapas and a nice wine list.

FESTIVALS AND RIOJA

Spaniards stop dead in their tracks for festivals. There is a total cessation of their daily routine; it is equivalent to a North American snow day. But festivals can go on for days, as if the snowstorm had turned into a blizzard. Festivals in Spain are passionate and steeped in many hundreds of years of tradition. They are a true claim to fame. No other country celebrates life with such grandeur.

The most famous festival in Rioja is San Mateo, the wine harvest festival; it begins on September 21 with the feast of San Mateo (Saint Matthew) and continues for five more days.

The soul of the city is so involved with the region's wine industry that the pavement on some sidewalks is embossed with bunches of grapes. For San Mateo the water in one of the many fountains that punctuate the Gran Vía, a major boulevard near the Old Quarter, is dyed the color of red wine.

The festivities begin in the Paseo del Espolón, a central tree-lined park. Young girls dressed in traditional Riojan costumes carry baskets of grapes that they pour into a vat. After two costumed men join arms and stomp the grapes, the first must is placed in a jug that is handed to the Vendimiadores, who are the prince and princess of the festival. They then offer it to a statue of the patron saint of La Rioja, Our Lady of Valvanera.

But the festival really takes over all of Logroño, especially the Old Quarter dominated by the Baroque spires of the Cathedral of Santa María de la Redonda. One custom is parades of costumed characters with giant heads; called the Cabezudos, they range from priests to kings and matadors. The costumes make some of the figures at least ten feet tall, and with them come musicians and dancers.

Music is central to this celebration. There are small bands of musicians wandering the streets and organized bands similar to the krewes of New Orleans marching through the city after the bullfights each night in resplendent uniforms. There are free concerts from afternoon until late in the evening. The tapas bars are bustling all day long, toasting with the wine from previous harvests.

HARO

Haro, a small city with about 12,000 residents, is the heart and soul of the Rioja Alta subregion. Wine is so integrated into the fabric of life there that its patron saint is honored with a Battle of Wine (*Batalla del Vino*) in late June each year (see page 42).

The reasons to go to Haro are plentiful, but the best of all is the concentration of world-class centenary wineries, all within walking distance; they were built after the completion of the train station in 1880. Between 1868 and 1902, eighteen bodegas were established in Rioja, and ten of them were in Haro. They are all there—great wines to drink today or allow to age for years or even decades. In just one day it would be easy to stock a cellar.

In 1900 Haro had established the greatest concentration of bodegas in Rioja, and it was—with Paris and London—in the elite group of cities in Europe that could boast of having electricity. Haro was a city made rich from wine. It was the site of the Bank of Spain, and every corner had either a bank or a jewelry shop.

BELOW AND OPPOSITE: Bodegas Bilbaínas

HARO'S FAMED BATTLE OF WINE

The Battle of Wine takes place on the feast day of Saint Peter, which is one of the most celebrated in Spain. In Rioja several pilgrimages became established on saints' days, including one to the sixth-century home site of San Felices in Bilibio as a result of his importance as the teacher and mentor of the revered San Millán, who had a central role in the history of this region (see page 56). This pilgrimage had taken place for centuries, but it was in the 1800s that a bit of Spanish spirit entered in, and trekkers began splattering one another with wine. It took until 1949, however, for the region's daily newspaper, *La Rioja*, to dub it the Battle of Wine.

As is the case with all Spanish festivals, regular life comes to a screeching halt on the day of the Battle of Wine. It is also typical that the festival embraces many generations. The night before the battle, local bistros and bars are packed with Riojans and foreigners celebrating together before beginning the 4-mile (6-kilometer) walk to Bilibio the next morning.

Modern-day pilgrims make their way down the road and up the hill to Bilibio, squirted occasionally with wine, en route to a tiny old chapel excavated from the mountain and adjoining a monument to San Felices. After the sermon, churchgoers are blasted with red wine by their friends and neighbors, either winemakers or those who have obtained grape must from local winemakers. In fact, anyone who is able to obtain wine brings it—along with all manner of pressure pumps and toy guns. Participants also bring picnics to consume between wine battles, and strolling musicians provide accompaniment to this day of fun before the purple warriors straggle back to Haro.

NÁJERA

The pilgrims' road to Santiago de Compostela runs west from Logroño to Nájera, a town of about nine thousand on the Najerilla River. The village is enchanting, beginning with the romantic bridge one crosses to enter it.

The town's name was given to it by the Moors; King Ordoño II of Leon conquered Nájera for Navarre in 923, and the town was that kingdom's capital until 1054, when Nájera was absorbed into Castile after the Battle of Atapuerca. As in many Spanish towns, the Moorish influence remained. Later in the eleventh century, the French abbot Peter the Venerable is said to have made Nájera his home base while commissioning translations of important Islamic works, including the first translation of the Koran.

The eleventh-century church of Santa María la Real was an important burial spot for Spanish monarchs. Built as a royal fortress, it was ceded to the Cluniac order in 1079. The church was constructed on a spot where, legend has it, a statue of the Virgin Mary was discovered in a cave, which can still be seen within the church. A stop on the Camino de Santiago, Santa María la Real is best known for the sixteenth-century woodwork in the choir. In the Pantheon are the tombs of twelve Spanish monarchs, and the Knight's Cloister (*Claustro de los Caballeros*) combines several architectural styles, including ornate filigree Gothic.

AGRICULTURE IN LA RIOJA

The seven rivers that enter the Ebro on its right bank create a climate and gentle irrigation that not only nurture grapes but also allow crops to grow to a vibrant color and sumptuous flavor. In Riojan cuisine this bounty from the earth is treated simply. The red peppers are simply grilled, drizzled with extra-virgin olive oil, and sprinkled with garlic: they are one the region's delicacies.

Crops are so important in La Rioja that many have been granted Protected Designation of Origin (PDO), meaning that no other region or country can claim to produce that crop. One of these, as of 2002, was the large green Pera de Rincón de Soto, the only pear to receive such a designation. Pears have grown on this land for centuries; the first historical reference to the "exquisite fruit" dates to 1747, and pears were a favorite in the court of King Philip V at that time.

Another fruit of note in La Rioja, in both its fresh and dried forms, is the plum. The more than 950 acres (388 hectares) of the central and eastern parts of the region devoted to these fruit trees of the Claudia Reina Verde variety are all picked by hand. There are now more than a hundred growers whose products are marketed under the label Ciruela de Nalda y Quel, which is a guaranteed mark of quality for both plums and prunes from the region.

Sweet Marcona almonds and intensely flavored walnuts with the designation Nuez de Pedroso are other tree crops for which La Rioja is known.

Ground crops also create a cornucopia of colorful and nutritious options. Small heads of cauliflower (coliflor) from Calahorra are known for their snowy whiteness and well-formed green leaves. Calahorra cauliflower is given a Protected Geographical Indication (PGI) as assurance of its provenance, as are the region's red peppers (pimientos Riojanos). This native variety, Najerano, is grown on small plots, and 70 percent of the harvest is roasted and sold in tins.

Mushrooms from La Rioja are the most numerous in Spain, and the crop is second only to grapes in terms of importance. About 3 percent of the world's mushrooms are grown in La Rioja. Since 2006, the mushrooms have been protected by a Marca de Garantía, which covers five distinct species. The mushrooms are grown and processed under strict regulations and are marketed under the label Champiñones y Setas de La Rioja.

Thick stalks of succulent white asparagus transcend regional boundaries and are named for the neighboring region of Navarre. The harvest is a mere two weeks long, and the crop of espárragos is rushed to processors to retain the stalks' sweetness once canned or jarred. But if one is lucky enough to be in Rioja in May when the harvest is taking place, they can be savored fresh and are a true delicacy.

OPPOSITE: Santa María la Real
FOLLOWING PAGES: The Najerilla Valley at Hormilla

CAMERANO CHEESE

Camerano cheese, another product given a PDO, has been made in La Rioja since the eleventh century from the milk of goats that roamed between the mountains and the valleys in search of grass. Today, cheese production is centered in the Cameros Mountains and the goats are raised in the nearby Leza Valley.

Traditionally the cheese was made in wicker molds called *cillas*, which gave the exterior an etched appearance; molds with a similar pattern are used today. The cheeses are flat and cylindrical and generally weigh about 2 pounds (1 kilogram). The interior of a fresh cheese is a bright white mass without holes. The texture is smooth, and the flavor falls between sweet and acidic. It is milky, fatty, and easily melted and can be eaten as dessert when drizzled with honey.

LA RIOJA'S EXTRAORDINARY OLIVE OIL

The soil of Spain supports more than 300 million olive trees covering more than 23 square miles (60 square kilometers). Only tending vines and growing grains are more important in La Rioja than harvesting olives and pressing olive oil. In the last decade the number of brands of olive oil from La Rioja has skyrocketed from less than a half dozen to more than forty. Like their neighbors making wine, the olive oil producers bottle oil of high quality in small quantities from Arbequina and Empeltre (also called Ibizan) olives, which produce a very fruity oil, and Picual olives, which produce oil with a more assertive flavor.

The olive groves are concentrated in the Cidacos and Alhama Valleys, where the harvest takes place from October to January, and the fruit is transported to presses throughout La Rioja. Olive oil is regulated in La Rioja with the Denomination of Origin, which applies to the extra-virgin oils produced, processed, and packaged in the region. Each and every aspect of the processes and techniques used to produce the oil is specifically aimed to showcase its intense green color and fruity flavor. The use of genetically modified species is prohibited. With an annual production of 500,000 liters, the oil is sold by thirty-eight national and international brands.

CLEMENTE BEA
AND RIHUELO FARM'S
"BEA" OLIVE OIL

Raised in Rioja Baja as the son of a farmer who cultivated fruit trees when most of his neighbors raised beets, Clemente Bea studied to be a veterinarian, and his "day job" is inspecting meat production facilities in the region. But his true passion is cultivating olive groves at the base of the Yerga Mountains, the result of which is Bea Extra-Virgin Olive Oil from Arbequina olives, a variety he and many of La Rioja's producers believe adapts well to the region's excellent soil, which is rich with mineral salts. His groves are about a half mile from the paved road, and one passes through acres of vineyards as well as fig and pear trees to reach them. When he speaks of his olive groves, an aura of passion and energy infuses his every word and physical gesture.

The company is made up of Clemente and his wife, along with his sister, Magüi Bea. They describe their "project" as one to "restore the prestige of growing and production of high-quality olive oil in the region of La Rioja." To accomplish this goal, they combine technological innovation with time-honored cultivation methods. The oil is bottled and corked like a fine wine.

They are obviously succeeding at their mission. Their oil, which has both ecological and organic certifications, has an intense bouquet of freshly cut grass and fruit flavors on the palate. It also has been the recipient of many international awards since 2000, including some given in Italy, Spain's rival in olive oil.

MONASTERIES, MYSTICS, AND MOUNTAINS

2

Certain facets of the topography and history of Rioja differentiate this region from others, not only on the Iberian Peninsula but also among the world's other great wine-producing areas. These lands have supported and nourished vineyards for more than a millennium. The serendipitous history of these plantings stems from the evolution of monasteries founded to pay homage to one man: San Millán.

San Millán traditionally is portrayed as an extraordinary person who inspired those around him during his life and generations of those who followed him after his death. He also holds a place of paramount importance in the development of Rioja's wine industry. The village bearing his name, San Millán de la Cogolla, is home to not one but two monasteries noted over the centuries as havens for spiritual intelligence, intellectual values, and extensive libraries. The monasteries remain surrounded by vineyards.

The legends surrounding San Millán drew many mystics during subsequent centuries to live in caves carved from the area's mountains. At the same time, the mountains play a pivotal role in developing the spirit of Rioja and its wines as their jagged topography creates microclimates, all with rich soil, that sustain old and new vines alike.

These three components—the monasteries, the mystics, and the mountains—create a picturesque setting where Rioja's history and spirit come alive. They are part of the heritage of the people and their wines.

CHAPTER OPENER: Suso Monastery
PREVIOUS PAGES: The Village of San Millán de la Cogolla
PREVIOUS RIGHT TOP AND BOTTOM: Tomb of San Millán
at Suso Monastery
RIGHT: Yuso Monastery

THE LIFE AND LASTING LEGACY OF SAN MILLÁN

San Millán's life was documented almost from the time of his death. This pivotal figure in Spanish history was born in Rioja in 473 and died in 574. Living for more than a century could be considered a miracle in itself by contemporary standards of longevity, let alone in the sixth century.

San Millán was a shepherd who at the age of twenty experienced a spiritual calling that led him to study under San Felices in Bilibio, a small village near Haro. He sought San Felices's counsel, wisdom, and teachings to understand the direction of the mission he felt compelled to follow.

After his ordination he spent a short time as a priest in the church at Berceo. According to legend, he soon became disenchanted with the daily routine mandated for the clergy. At the same time, his peers considered him a nonconformist because of his generosity to the poor. It was by mutual agreement, therefore, that he abandoned parish work and began forty years of life as a hermit in the Cárdenas River valley. He dedicated his days primarily to prayer and penance and provided help to those who asked; he became known for his service to the needy.

Atypically for his era, however, San Millán, known affectionately as Emiliano, appealed to a range of socioeconomic groups; he was sought after by the rich as well as the poor. His intercession was sought by kings and counts to ensure victory in battle even long after his death.

They apparently credited him for their successes, especially in the wars against the Moors; he was named patron saint of Castile and Navarre and thereafter of all of Christian Spain.

It was their devotion to San Millán that served as inspiration for troops during the reconquest of Spain from the Moors, which ended in 1492, more than nine hundred years after his death. His spiritual role as a protector in battle may be the reason he often is portrayed on horseback fighting the Moors, although he was never a soldier. In this respect comparisons can be drawn to similar depictions of Saint James.

Word of San Millán's miracles spread, and he attracted fellow hermits who settled in neighboring caves. Periodically they would meet to pray together, and their meeting place was incorporated into the site of the Suso monastery; as Suso became a community, the isolated life of hermits was replaced with the communal one of monks.

Most historical records of this antiquity have been lost or remain undiscovered, but we have accurate information on the life of San Millán—this, too, could be deemed miraculous. San Millán's five disciples—Citonato, Geroncio, Sofronio, Anselo, and Potamia—all wrote journals dealing with his life in about 613. These writings became the basis for the seminal documentation of his life written in Latin in 635 by San Braulio, born in the seventh century shortly after San Millán's death. It was from this text that Gonzalo Berceo penned his *Vida de San Millán* (Life of Saint Millán) in 1234 in what had by then evolved into the Castilian language.

OPPOSITE: Ivory Reliquary of San Millán at Yuso Monastery

THE MONASTERIES THAT GREW AROUND THE MAN: SUSO AND YUSO

The monastic community was crucial in the development of viniculture in Rioja, and that community centered on the two monasteries built to honor San Millán: Suso and Yuso. The words mean "upper" and "lower" in archaic Castilian and refer to the monasteries' relative positions in the mountains.

The ninth century in Rioja was characterized by an influx of San Millán's followers. Until the arrival of monks seeking his teachings, the Riojan landscape consisted of mountain ranges, grazing pastures for sheep, and vibrant green forests filled with Holm Oak (an evergreen species native to the Mediterranean region) and mushrooms.

The Benedictine monks brought a strong work ethic and began to plow the pastures, cut down the trees, and sow and plant. They sowed wheat, barley, and hay but planted only grapevines. By the end of the tenth century, vineyards were part of the landscape, and there were many workers to tend them. The laws of Navarre stipulated that if a worker left the community, his home and inheritance would become the property of the monastery. Setting aside questions of right and wrong, this law no doubt provided a strong incentive to stay.

This colonization continued for four centuries, producing the greatest physical alternation of the region in its history. By the tenth century this beautiful fabled valley sandwiched between the kingdoms of Navarre and Castile was already a destination of note. Even pilgrims on the route to Santiago de Compostela often detoured from Nájera to San Millán on foot, a mere 12 miles (20 kilometers) in a journey totaling hundreds of miles, and picked up the route again in the village of Azofra.

Within the walls of the monasteries the days were governed by the sun, the moon, and the seasons, which jointly determined the start of a day, the end of a day, sleep, planting, and harvesting. Grains such as millet and wheat were defined by either short or long cycles, and the vines' journey carefully moved with the four seasons in alignment with the four corners of the cloister. Contemplation and prayer were practiced by walking the pattern of the quadrant of the cloister. The principles of what we know today as biodynamic farming were naturally woven into the history of Rioja's vines. Sheep manure, wildflowers, and herbs were mixed into the already rich soil. It is enlightening to see how the modern-day term *biodynamic* employs practices guided by Mother Earth and honored by the human hand so many centuries ago.

Communal mealtime was sacred and always included wine; expulsion from the table was the worst punishment a monk could endure. After the sun set, evenings were filled with choral singing and chanting to end the day with vibration, sound, and rhythm.

The monasteries were the only educational institutions in Spain until the thirteenth century. Although not ultimately committed to monastic life, the

OPPOSITE: Suso Monastery

sons of the nobility were educated alongside the monks. In Rioja, teaching methods were highly personalized, with only a few students assigned to a master.

MONASTERY OF SUSO

Situated at the end of the Sierra de la Demanda mountain range, the tiny village of San Millán de la Cogolla is in the flattest area of Rioja. Although the village is not otherwise noteworthy, the two monasteries it contains are central to the history of the region.

The formation of the first monastery, Suso, was accomplished in a very unorthodox fashion for tenth-century Spain. Typically, during that era a monastic community would acquire land and then construct a monastery complex as donations accumulated in its coffers. But monks were so inspired by the life of San Millán that his grave site became a destination for worship. Moved by this grassroots outpouring from the clergy and further motivated by the opportunity to position themselves on the right bank of the Ebro, Queen Doña Toda of Navarre and her son, García Sánchez III, decided to build a monastery at San Millán's cave and grave site. This building was erected in only three years, between 931 and 934. The monarchs gave the monastery and the surrounding hillsides and pastures to the monks.

The feeling of the building is ancient. It has a very simple exterior made from the pink-toned stone of the surrounding mountains and a tile roof of the same hue. Visitors enter through a narrow passageway lined with the tombs of kings and queens, all of which are unadorned. The interior contains vaulted arches in three styles, with the largest number being Mozarabic, an influence also reflected in the complex tile work. The overwhelming emotional impact of the Suso monastery comes from viewing the hermit caves integrated into the structure and forming a series of small chapels around its perimeter. These caves, with sections excavated for sleeping as well as praying, show the devotion inspired by this simple saint.

From its location at the top of a mountain, the monastery also offers spectacular views of the surrounding region and forests of evergreen trees. It is truly a luminous place.

The Suso monastery benefited from its position between the kingdoms of Navarre and Castile and received donations from both monarchies. In a spirit of unsubtle competition, the nobility in subsequent generations continued to match and double the donations of their monarchs, neighbors, and ancestors. After the establishment of the Suso monastery, other kings, queens, and counts quickly donated churches as they built their personal castles and villas in the region surrounding the monastery.

ABOVE: Tomb of San Millán
OPPOSITE: Cloister at Yuso Monastery

By 956, García Sánchez III, now king of Navarre, established his court in the enchanting village of Nájera and granted its church to the jurisdiction of the Suso monastery. In a short time Nájera would amass a strong concentration of vineyards, and within fifty years the San Millán monastery's acquisitions extended to the Cantabrian Sea almost 100 miles (150 kilometers) away.

MONASTERY OF YUSO

Legend states that in 1053 a procession led by the Navarrese King García de Nájera (García V), accompanied by a group of bishops, was descending from Suso to take the stone coffers containing the remains of San Millán to the recently founded monastery of Santa María la Real in Nájera.

After winding down more than a mile of steep hairpin turns on the narrow road from the peak where Suso is situated, all those present witnessed the oxen and accompanying animals halt in their tracks at the foot of the mountain. Standing at the base of the San Lorenzo Mountains, the highest peaks in Rioja at more than 7,200 feet (2,200 meters), they tried to move the recalcitrant animals, but the oxen refused to budge despite numerous attempts.

Simultaneously exasperated and enlightened, King García decided to construct a new monastery at the site, and Yuso was consecrated in 1067. At about that

time great masters created coffers from ivory, gold, and precious stones for the remains of San Millán and his teacher, San Felices. Both are great works of decorative art and remain on exhibit at Yuso.

Although built in a classically Romanesque style in the eleventh century, the Yuso monastery was destroyed in a fire and rebuilt in the sixteenth century as an example of High Renaissance architecture and decoration; it was completed by the eighteenth century.

The wealth and power of both monasteries are reflected in Yuso's grandeur, decor, library, archives, and furnishings. Considered a conservative and Visigothic monastery, Yuso became known for the strong intellectual tradition of the Benedictine order and for its extensive library. Although ransacked during the Napoleonic Wars in the nineteenth century and abandoned at different points during the twentieth century, the Yuso library and archives hold over 10,000 volumes of fascinating works, all bound in leather and housed in cabinets. In 1878, the Augustine order took occupancy of the monastery and remains there today, having endured more than four decades of pain during the Spanish Civil War and the Franco regime.

Of the 209 monasteries in Spain, only 7 are deemed truly significant, and the Yuso monastery is the only one in Rioja listed in that group. It was proclaimed a UNESCO World Heritage Site in 1997.

LEFT: Sacristy at Yuso Monastery
OPPOSITE: Altarpiece, Cathedral of Santo Domingo de la Calzada

THE MYSTICS

Rioja's collection of saints is diverse. Often referred to as hermits, they were individuals of isolation, poverty, courage, and humility. Until the development of Romance languages such as Spanish and French, Latin was used for both verbal and written communication. In Latin, the word for humility is *humus*. Its meaning in Latin approximates "earthly and grounded," which is indeed reflective of these individuals and their life's work.

Whether they are referred to as hermits, saints, mystics, or priests, one thing is certain: they were spiritual, highly conscious people. They were also productive. They fought to conquer the Moors at the same time that they oversaw the building of bridges and roadways to ease the pilgrims' journey.

In the vast mountains of Rioja these hermits excavated caves that became their homes. Although the caves at Suso are now within the walls of the monastery, the largest concentration of hermit cave sites is in the Yerga Mountains of Rioja Baja, which have some of the highest elevations in Rioja. These gave rise to the first monastery of the Cistercian Order, built between 1185 and 1247 in what is technically Navarre. The Fitero monastery is on the Alhama River there and has been a national monument since 1931.

These contemplative masters excavated their home sites with patience and persistence, and these qualities remain part of the Riojan spirit. Even Rioja's signature Gran Reserva wines reflect patience, as they must be aged in bodegas for at least five years.

Each mystic added his or her history to the region's lore. One such mystic, Santo Domingo, born in 1019, inspired great stories that became legends throughout medieval Europe. He was responsible for creating an entire town and built its bridges to ensure a pathway for pilgrims on the Camino de Santiago. In addition to being spiritual, these mystics were pragmatists—and industrious ones at that.

The story of the rooster and the hen in Santo Domingo was considered one of the greatest miracles of the era. According to legend, to signal that a boy who had been hanged was still alive, the saint caused the two birds, which were already cooked, to jump from their pans and sing. To honor the miracle, to this day a cock and a hen are placed on the regal altarpiece of the twelfth-century Romanesque cathedral named for Santo Domingo.

THE MOUNTAINS

The peaks stand in silence, but it is a silence that speaks. Ranges such as the Cantabrian, San Lorenzo, Obarenes, Yerga, and Toloño provide the same scenery they did more than a thousand years ago and continue to stand secure, protecting their treasured vines and valleys and manifesting their beauty, serenity, and power for all to see. Riojan literature and sayings include frequent references to the mountains and describe them with words such as *steady, anchored, stuck*, and *stationary*. Ernest Hemingway evoked the weather-giving mountains in *For Whom the Bell Tolls.* Snow comes over one range, severe dry cold over another. Riojans today look to these ranges to predict what nature will bring.

Rioja's majestic mountains stand with masculine force. The mountains' role as a barrier or shield has been significant throughout the history of the region. They provided trusted shelter in the lives of the numerous hermits and saints who lived in them. One thousand years later, they hid and aided fighters during the Spanish Civil War. Today they shield the vineyards and valleys on their lee sides from the winds of the Atlantic and Mediterranean, as they have done for centuries. Aside from Rioja's thousand-year reputation as a hospitable region with good people, its vast mountain ranges add a veil of security to one's sensory experience in this land. One finds oneself in a state of comfort in their presence.

RIGHT: **Alesanco in the Autumn**

THE WINE REGION OF RIOJA

3

Many new world wine regions have emerged as a result of the largesse of New World fortunes; vineyards have been planted in every climate in which grapes can be made to grow. However, in the Old World, in regions such as Rioja that are steeped in thousands of years of grape-growing history, the vines speak a language of tradition and heritage created by nature's design.

When the various elements of the *Denominación de Origen Calificada* (DOCa) Rioja's vineyards are analyzed by their history, land, and climate, and the wisdom of many generations of Riojan winemakers is factored in, it is not surprising that within a small area—a mere 30 miles (48 kilometers) wide by 70 miles (112 kilometers) long— some of the greatest Old World wines are made. Although there is a rich heritage, Rioja is a vibrant contemporary region, too. In the last 15 years more new bodegas have been founded than in the previous 150 years.

All of Rioja's vineyards are in the Ebro River valley or the valleys of its tributaries, but their soil and character vary greatly. Some grapes are grown on the terraced slopes of alluvial plains, and others benefit from the iron-rich soils at mountain heights. The vineyards of Rioja extend in places outside the boundaries of La Rioja and into the neighboring provinces, but grapes are wiser than governments. All these lands constitute the Rioja we know today, and the Rioja Regulatory Control Board oversees all production regardless of provincial affiliation.

CHAPTER OPENER: Vineyard in Hormilla
PREVIOUS PAGES: Rioja Baja Vineyard and Vines
RIGHT: Sierra Cantabria Vines

70

EVOLUTION OF A WINE REGION

Viticulture has existed in Rioja for thousands of years. The ancient Phoenicians, who traveled up the Ebro and settled in what is now the Rioja Baja subregion near Alfaro, planted grapes in the eleventh century BCE. The Romans also made wine there, as they did in most of the great Old World wine regions that fell under their domination. Vineyards were established in the second century BCE near what we know today as Logroño and Calahorra.

The wine historian Roger Dion has written that it is likely that when the Romans settled in the Bordeaux region a century after they arrived in Rioja, the vine cuttings they brought to Bordeaux were from Rioja. This ancient *Balisca* species may have engendered Cabernet Sauvignon, Cabernet Franc, and Merlot just as it is the predecessor of Tempranillo and Garnacha.

It is known that the arrival of monks following in the footsteps of San Millán allowed vineyards to become firmly established in Rioja. The story of how the vine—and wine—took hold in Rioja is told by references in texts almost as old as the saint himself and in subsequent historical records of kingdoms, taxes, and the wool industry.

Before the tenth century in Rioja vines were planted primarily at altitudes much higher than they are today. In 981, according to records, new vines were planted next to

LEFT: Spring Vines in Briones

existing old vines. It also is known that vine cultivation was strong from the ninth century onward. The average size of a parcel was a little more than half an acre (2,500 square meters); parcels were densely planted, and fruit trees were dispersed throughout the vineyards.

The expansion of vineyards and crops of cereal grains formed a strong foundation for the region's economy. Even in that early era, vine cultivation was far more labor-intensive than was growing cereal grains. However, tools created from iron mined from nearby mines in the Alavesa were useful in the vineyard. Texts from this era also detail viticultural practices such as pruning and the location of various vineyards.

By the eleventh century, production of wine and wheat was strong in Rioja, and the growth surge during this century can be credited to Castile. In 1067, during the region's ongoing border disputes, the kingdoms of Castile and Navarre united as Castile. This merger was critical, and by 1076 the monastery of San Millán officially belonged to Castile. There were local laws dictating that the king's vineyards be harvested before any others, and this guarantee of status and accompanying prosperity prompted the planting of additional vines.

Castile's rulers were savvy businessmen, as the world would discover a few centuries later when they financed the exploration of the New World. King Alfonso VI of Castile (1040–1109) stimulated trade between the

DOCA AND QUALITY

Since the twelfth century, when King Sancho of Navarre officially recognized the wines of Rioja, it has been desirable to protect the quality of those wines and keep outsiders from claiming to make an equal product. Efforts to this end culminated in the twentieth century, when the word *Rioja* was legally added to wine labels to signify a sort of branding for the first time in 1925. In 1926 Rioja wines were given a *Denominación de Origen* (DO), guaranteeing that wines that claimed to be Rioja were actually produced in the region, and complied with regulations specifying the varieties of grapes that could be used, the grape yield per hectare, winemaking and aging methods, and labeling. In the same year a control board, the predecessor of the Rioja Regulatory Control Board, was created to issue guarantee seals for the wines and enforce quality.

In 1991, Rioja was the first Spanish wine region to be granted a DOCa in place of its DO, based on sustained high quality over a long period. There are only two such regions in Spain—Priorat is the other—but there are many DO wines from Spain's quality wine regions, each with unique grape-growing and winemaking regulations that ensure specific quality. Similar quality systems exist in other European wine regions.

San Millán monasteries and neighboring regions, which were also Castile's territories. Hence, the Ebro River was used efficiently and effectively for the transport of wool, wine, and wood.

Documented records show that the majority of proceeds from lucrative wool sales were channeled into vineyard expansion and only secondarily into additional wheat fields. Vineyards, wheat fields, and sheep guaranteed food for the region's population, which was composed primarily of monks, soldiers, and Riojan villagers. From the late eleventh century onward, vineyard records are accessible and plentiful. They reveal much about the local laws and document contracts establishing significant vineyard plantings in enchanting historical villages such as Cañas, Alesanco, Tricio, and Nájera.

By the twelfth century wine had acquired great commercial value for Rioja and its rulers. Vineyards were taxed at a much lower rate than wheat fields or pasturelands, providing a financial incentive to increase their acreage. Additionally, there was a law requiring mandatory community service; each villager had to work the harvest at least one day per harvest.

The vast numbers of churches under the ownership of the San Millán monasteries needed wine to celebrate the Eucharist. Fortuitously, at the same time the nobility chose wine as its beverage of choice over the traditional cider. The power base of vineyards and wine therefore had both a divine and an economic role. This power base was firmly seated in the San Millán mother monastery: Throughout the medieval era, 90 percent of the vines in Rioja were owned by that monastery and only 10 percent were controlled by the other eleven monasteries and convents in the region. This consolidated ownership strengthened the wine industry because monasteries of the same order had internal systems of communication that allowed them to share information on vineyard care and vinification techniques. Single ownership also allowed for consistent vine cultivation, control, and experimentation at a time when kingdoms and lands changed hands frequently.

By the thirteenth century, when exportation of red wine, white wine, and often a blend of the two to England began, the wines of Rioja were already known and popular in both Castile and the Basque Country. Mid-thirteenth-century documents detailing wine routes in Europe show Bilbao as the only stop in Spain before the wine moved on to England.

In spite of the dramatic development of the vineyards in medieval times, it was only at the end of the fifteenth century and the beginning of the sixteenth that Rioja found lasting political unification, again under the rule of Castile. This brought great stability to the region; its population doubled, and the wine-growing areas expanded toward Logroño, well beyond their medieval boundaries. However, the wool industry remained the most commercially profitable enterprise during those centuries.

In the late eighteenth century the amount of land under cultivation reached one of its historical highs. Wine production had grown to four times what it had been in the sixteenth century. Villages such as Labastida, Laguardia, Cenicero, San Vicente, and Haro all became thriving wine municipalities. It was during this era that the practice of aging wine in oak barrels began, which extended the longevity of the wine.

In the late nineteenth century the railroad arrived, and this boost to the infrastructure created the wine industry as we know it today. From Rioja, wines could travel to the nearby port city of Bilbao and then on to destinations around the world.

PESTS AND PROGRESS

Although the wines of Rioja undoubtedly would have been highly regarded on their own merit, two devastating "Trojan horses" brought from the United States to Europe created skyrocketing growth in the second half of the nineteenth century.

The first of these "plagues" was oidium, a powdery mildew that devastated the vineyards of Bordeaux in 1852 and then ravaged the vines in Galicia in northwestern Spain. Luckily, the vineyards in Rioja were only moderately afflicted, and their market share grew throughout Europe.

The second infestation, however, was much more severe. Grape phylloxera, an almost microscopically small insect related to the aphid, feeds on the roots or leaves of grapevines, depending on the species of the insect. Phylloxera has a complex life cycle, and each part of that cycle can destroy vines. It was introduced to Europe when avid English botanists returned home with vine cuttings from the United States.

The epidemic began in England and then crossed the English Channel to continental Europe. In 1863 it was detected in the Rhône, and soon thereafter in Bordeaux. It is estimated that between 70 percent and 90 percent of French vines became infected.

French winemakers in general and those from Bordeaux in particular flooded into nearby Rioja (today about a four-hour drive) in search of bulk grape juice to fulfill their orders. Their arrival in Rioja created a controversial sea change in the region.

This boom in Rioja lasted until the 1890s, when phylloxera infected the vines there, too. In the Rioja Alavesa only 882 acres (357 hectares) of the original 23,500 acres (9,509 hectares) survived in 1900. But the devastation in Rioja was of a shorter duration than that in France. By 1900 the French had discovered a solution; European vines were grafted onto American rootstock, which was resistant to phylloxera. The vintners in Rioja quickly followed that lead. Today, almost all European vines grow on American rootstocks for that reason.

RIGHT: Flowering Tempranillo

VICTOR CRUZ MANSO DE ZÚÑIGA

Many great Riojans have been at the helm of shaping the DOCa as we know it today. One of them was Victor Cruz Manso de Zúñiga, who led Rioja through phylloxera infestation. As the second director of the Rioja Enological Station in Haro, he served a twenty-eight-year term, from 1893 to 1921.

Zúñiga is revered for many achievements during his tenure. His papers, collected and preserved in the library of the Rioja Enological Station today, reference communication with the great viticulturists and enologists of his time, including Pierre Marie Alexis Millardet, a botanist and plant pathologist; Gaston Fouex, a scientist at the University of Montpellier; and Louis Ravaz, an expert on the propagation of vines. Zúñiga was familiar with Louis Pasteur´s work on alcoholic fermentation. He created a curriculum in enology that made the station an educational facility. Scholars reference his research papers to this day.

More than a century ago, Zúñiga was a proponent of the indigenous Graciano grape despite the challenges it presented to growers rather than the Cabernet Sauvignon favored by the French. It was he who created the first blend of 75 percent Tempranillo, 15 percent Garnacha, and 10 percent Mazuelo, which is still used today for many Rioja wines intended for aging.

His greatest achievement, however, was his consummate leadership in combating phylloxera in Rioja. He detected the pest in 1899 in the Traslaventa and Royo Lázaro vineyards in the municipality of Sajazarra in the Rioja Alta. About 85 percent of the vines were destroyed, and the people of the region were understandably panicked. Zúñiga's patience and intelligence guided everyone through the devastation. He then oversaw replanting, a task completed by 1908.

He also supported and worked closely with Don Rafael López de Heredia Landeta, the great-grandfather of the current winemaker Mercedes López de Heredia, on the postphylloxera replanting plan for his Viña Tondonia vineyard in 1913.

Today the Zúñiga family owns the same property it did a century ago in the village of Torremontalbo in the Najerilla Valley. Victor's great-grandnephew, Íñigo Manso de Zúñiga, obtained a master's degree in enology in Bordeaux in 1983. He is an accomplished winemaker who has worked in various DO regions of Spain, but his reverence for Rioja and the wines he makes there is high. He works with prephylloxera vines more than a hundred years old growing in a corner of the Najerilla Valley. His great-granduncle planted those vines during the phylloxera epidemic and chose the site for its sandy soil, which was known to be inhospitable to the pest. Many dedicated Riojans like the Zúñiga family have shaped this region.

DIVERSE CLIMATE
IN A
SMALL REGION

If one could look at Rioja from outer space it would look like a long bowl; this is the depression of the Ebro River valley. The Ebro meanders through Rioja for 74 miles (120 kilometers) and becomes the spinal cord for the cluster of vineyards.

Crucial to viticulture in Rioja is the role played by the mountain ranges on either side of the Ebro as well as the two bodies of water—the Atlantic Ocean and the Mediterranean Sea—that form Spain's more than 3,000 miles (4,800 kilometers) of coastline. These geographic elements strongly affect the climate of Rioja.

To the north, the Sierra de Cantabria range protects the vineyards of the Rioja Alta and Rioja Alavesa subregions (see pages 84 and 92) from the strong Atlantic winds to the west and the winds from the Bay of Biscay to the north that otherwise would create an unforgiving climate. The Sierra de la Demanda and Sierra de Cameros ranges serve as a buffer against the strong southwestern winds for those regions. The soft autumn sprinkles coming off the mountains gently mist these regions. Early spring sunshine leads to a long, hot summer and a mild autumn as the harvest progresses. During the winter these highlands experience snow and freezing temperatures, and these help wipe out insects that cannot live through frosts.

The climate of the Rioja Baja, which is the subzone closest to the Mediterranean, is warmer because of the air currents coming off that body of water, except in the highlands of the Yerga Mountains, which reach altitudes of 1,600 to 2,300 feet (500 to 700 meters). Vintages in Rioja Baja can vary greatly from those of Rioja Alta; this is important to know with the current growth of subzonal and single vineyard wines (see page 144).

Rainfall in Rioja varies little from one end of the region to the other; both Haro and Logroño receive about 15 inches (400 millimeters) of rain a year. Alfaro, in Rioja Baja, receives slightly less. But in the highlands of Rioja Alta the rainfall can be almost double this amount.

Part of a region's overall climate, but often quite different from it, is each vineyard's subclimate, called the mesoclimate. (There is an even smaller subclimate within each grapevine called the microclimate.) The individual vineyard's climate is also related to geographic features, such as the slope of the vineyard, which affects the exposure of the vines to the sunlight; the protective influence of hills or forests; the warming and humidifying influence of lakes; and elevation, which affects temperature and rainfall in specific sites. In Rioja both the climate and mesoclimate are extraordinarily diverse. Whereas the climate makes certain regions ideal for grape growing, mesoclimate and soil structure make certain plots of land perfect for vineyards.

OPPOSITE: Jubera River Gorge at Robres del Castillo

THE TERROIR OF RIOJA

The term *terroir* (tare-**wahr**) describes the climate plus the nature of the soils and subsoils of a region and of individual vineyards. Meandering through Rioja, one can appreciate the outward aspects of its terroir from the landscape. There are jagged mountain ranges, slopes, hills, and bumps. The vineyards look like a mosaic or patchwork quilt of small parcels facing different directions, with rows of green separated by ribbons of intensely brown, rich soil. The amount of light and sun varies too, and the striking color contrast of the soils is captivating.

Just as no two terroirs in the world are alike, terroir in Rioja is unique to the region. Rioja is a singular place where nature provides the perfect cradle for people to create wines of superb quality. The terroir fits like a hand into the well-worn glove of the Tempranillo grape, the primary grape in this region. Terroir is not only regional, though; it exists on a vineyard level as well. For instance, Rioja wines are blends of grapes grown in all three of its subregions, but the winemakers are always aware of the terroir of the vineyards from which they are purchasing the grapes and the way it affects the flavor of the fruit.

It is terroir, which comes from the French word *terre,* meaning "earth," that gives all crops a sense of place; it creates a fingerprint of the earth on the grapes that comes through in their flavor characteristics and ultimately in the wine made from them. Mesoclimate, or vineyard climate, is one aspect of this elusive quality.

The temperature profile of a vineyard, the amount of rainfall it receives, and the typical proportion of sunlight to clouds all affect a vine's growth. The topography of a vineyard—its altitude and slope and its ability to drain after rainfall—is important. Geology is also important in terms of heat retention and light reflection. Rocks and soil can hold the heat of the day and radiate it during the night. Darker soils absorb and radiate heat better than do lighter soils. Stones on the surface of the ground also protect against evaporation of water from the soil beneath.

Other crops or wild plants grown near vineyards are also an element of terroir. Some tasters say that the mushrooms that thrive in Rioja's soils give a woodsy flavor to the region's red wines.

Terroir is the *living* component of a wine; it provides a stimulus that can ignite the passion of a winemaker. The vine is immobile; it is rooted in one place and mysteriously births its grapes from the water and minerals it sucks through its roots. The more ancient the region, the older the vineyard sites and the deeper the mystery. Wines that begin with unrivaled terroir speak for themselves; they are not designed to please a current trend, nor are they denatured because technology has taken over the process. The idea is that the more processes the wine undergoes, the less the terroir will make itself known in the wine. Limiting the amount of human interaction in winemaking allows the terroir to flavor the wine.

A GUIDE TO RIOJA'S THREE SUBREGIONS

The DOCa Rioja does not conform to political boundaries; the subregions are united by winemaking and by the Ebro running through them. The delineation of the subregions was one of the first acts of the Rioja Regulatory Control Board in 1926. This first control board was given the task of demarcating the Rioja production area, supervising the issuing of "guarantee seals," and recommending the legal measures to be taken against those who misappropriated or falsified the Rioja brand (see pages 145).

Despite changes in the grape varieties being planted and the increase in planting during the last twenty-five years, a significant factor that has remained constant is the pattern of land ownership. Today there are more than 120,000 registered parcels dispersed among more than 18,000 owners; the average size of a vineyard is about 1.3 acres (0.5 hectare). This creates the patchwork look of the landscape, as different growers intersperse their vines with other crops to suit their needs. But most important, the existence of thousands of small plots has an effect on the wines, because winemakers can pick and choose grapes from many vineyards based on the differing character of the fruit to create a well-balanced blend.

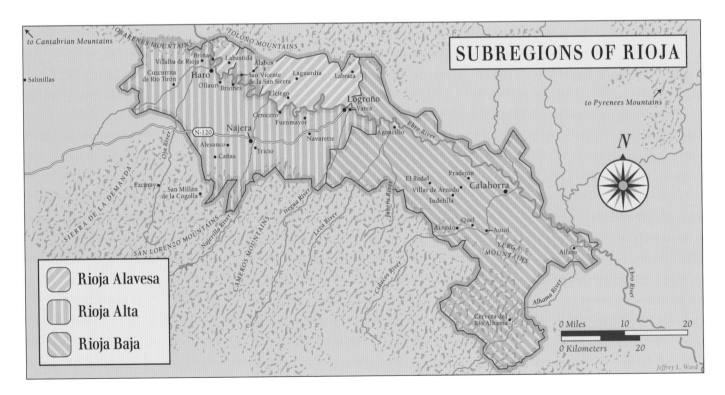

SUBREGIONS OF RIOJA

Rioja Alavesa
Rioja Alta
Rioja Baja

OPPOSITE: Hormilla

THE RIOJA ALTA

Rioja Alta translates as "High Rioja." Although its peaks are not substantially taller than those in the other two subregions, the region is situated higher up toward the headwaters of the Ebro River. The vineyards of the Rioja Alta represent 42 percent of those in the DOCa Rioja. Most of the region is on the right bank of the Ebro. In the Oja and Najerilla Valleys, however, a tongue of land that includes the towns of San Vicente de la Sonsierra and Abalos crosses to the left bank of the Ebro and is sandwiched between two areas of the Rioja Alavesa. The inclusion of this small pocket of land on the left bank

dates back to long before the demarcation of regions in the twentieth century. Sonsierra served as a stronghold for the kingdom of Navarre on the left bank of the Ebro but ultimately was won by Castile on the right bank. This geographic intersection speaks to the shared culture, grape varieties, and winemaking methods that caused the enological practices of Rioja Alta and Rioja Alavesa to evolve in such similar ways. Together the two subregions make a statement of solidarity about the meaning of Rioja wine.

The diversity of soil types is greater in the Rioja Alta than in either of the other two subregions. The Oja and Najerilla valley environments have different microclimates and soil characteristics. The most northwestern part of the DOCa and the Rioja Alta is the Oja Valley; it contains some of the highest peaks in Rioja and is subject to the greatest influence from the Atlantic Ocean. It includes such municipalities as Briñas, Briones, Haro, and Villalba de Rioja, whose vineyards contain a combination of chalky clay and alluvial soils, depending on their proximity to the river valleys. This area is home to many prized vineyards that grow grapes destined to produce Reservas and Gran Reservas—great wines intended for aging (see pages 131 and 132).

Also situated on the right bank, the Najerilla Valley contains a great percentage of the vines of the Rioja Alta. It lies to the north and south of the N-120 highway that connects the historic village of Nájera with Logroño. However, the vineyards on the left bank of the Ebro, where Ábalos, Briñas, and San Vicente de Sonsierra are

RIOJA ALTA

to Cantabrian Mountains

to Pyrenees Mountains

N

OBARENES MOUNTAINS

Ebro River

TOLOÑO MOUNTAINS

Briñas
Villalba de Rioja
Ábalos
Cuzcurrita del Rio Tirón
Haro
San Vicente de la Sonsierra
Ollauri
Briones

Najerilla River

Cenicero
Fuenmayor
Logroño
Varea
Ebro River

N-120
Alesanco
Navarrete
Nájera
Tricio

Iregua River

SIERRA DE LA DEMANDA

Oja River

Cañas

Ezcaray
San Millán de la Cogolla

CAMEROS MOUNTAINS

SAN LORENZO MOUNTAINS

0 Miles 5 10
0 Kilometers 20

Jeffrey L. Ward

located, are dominated by iron-rich clay soil similar to that of the Rioja Alavesa. In both subregions the Tempranillo grape dominates the plantings. This small sandwich of the Rioja Alta contains many inherited parcels of land that are used to grow old vines and are tended with methods that reflect strong family traditions.

CHOZOS

The Sonsierra area of the Rioja Alta, situated on the left bank of the Ebro, accounts for the greatest concentration of *chozos*, huts that historically provided shelter for the workers as they tended the grapes. Another name for these primarily round huts dotting the Riojan landscape is *guardaviñas* (guard-vines), and this is one aspect of what they originally were built for. If you have too much great Rioja wine at lunch (which is easy to do!), you may think you see Winnie the Pooh's ample backside sticking out of a *chozo* on the horizon. Or perhaps it is a distorted beehive or—better yet—a fort similar to the ones you dreamed of building during childhood.

Construction of *chozos* from sandstone and limestone began in the sixteenth century, and both their shape and their composition are unique to Rioja. They were a place to find comfort during inclement weather and to take naps during the intense work of the harvest; it was at least a one-hour walk from the vineyards to most villages. The *chozos* were also sheds for storing tools. During the weeks before harvest they would be occupied to protect the vineyards from being robbed. This practice

THE TREND TOWARD SITE-SPECIFIC MICROPLOTS

Today, without doubt, the winemakers of Rioja are in a state of evolution and are stretching themselves in pursuit of the finest production from their vineyards, using their seven indigenous grape varieties. The different soils and topography within very small areas have led to the exploration of the concept of site-specific microplots—identifying the strengths of each small parcel to focus the fruit better and allow greater creativity and control in building Rioja blends.

It is common for vineyards merely a mile apart to experience very different amounts of sun and rain as a result of their orientation. Soil composition also changes from vineyard to vineyard. As Óscar Tobía of Bodegas Tobía put it, "There are villages with great historic vineyards, but exploring the differences in altitude and orientation throughout the DOCa Rioja is where the challenge lies in the twenty-first century." This exploration of the potential of microplots creates enormous opportunities for the winemaker and stylistic diversity for the consumer. It will make terroir more important in the future, as it is today in other great red wine regions, such as Bordeaux, where grapes traditionally are crushed from just one estate or vineyard.

was especially important after phylloxera hit France and thieves would lurk to pilfer the vineyards at night. Another impetus for their initial construction was the territorial wars between the vintners and the shepherds during the sixteenth century as grapes began to dominate the landscape. The vines were taking over land formerly used for grazing sheep, and the shepherds were hardly happy about being evicted.

BRIONES

This ancient walled medieval village is now surrounded by such noted bodegas as Dinastía Vivanco and Allende. The first historical references to Briones go back to the time of the Romans; the old district, called Gimileo and now a separate wine village, took its name from Legio VII Gemina, the Roman legion that occupied the nearby city of León in the first century CE.

The village sits atop a steep hill more than 300 feet higher than the surrounding area, which gave it a strategic advantage over the centuries; it was passed from the control of Navarre to that of Castile many times. At the center of its main square is a house that dates from the fifteenth century; the buildings surrounding it were constructed up to the eighteenth century. The beige stone construction gives the village its sense of architectural unity.

It was in this historical setting that Rioja began to recoup its losses after the devastation of phylloxera (see page 75). In 1904 the village started the first postphylloxera school for the propagation of vines in the region.

OPPOSITE: *Chozo*
FOLLOWING PAGES: Briones on a Snowy Night

WHERE DID YOU STUDY?

There was a time when the greatest winemakers and viticulturists in Spain, known as agronomic engineers, went to study in prominent wine regions such as Bordeaux. Today, however, if you ask some of the most innovative and capable winemakers where they learned their art, many will reply that it was at the University of Rioja. Admission to the university's Department of Enology assures access to great minds that have an intimate knowledge of Rioja, its terroir, and its grapes.

Emilio Barco is revered for his meticulous accuracy and engaging style. Fernando Martínez de Toda has left his mark on students with his enthusiastic vineyard sojourns; he knows the vines of Rioja like he knows his own hand, and his teachings have become part of the way his students approach their careers. Joining these established masters at the University of Rioja is the adjunct professor Juan Carlos Sancha. The winemaker at Bodegas Ijalba for twenty years, he worked tirelessly as an advocate to rescue from obscurity indigenous grapes such as Maturana Tinta, Maturana Blanco, Graciano, and Tempranillo Blanco. He is also mentoring students to start what he terms "microbodegas," small winemaking facilities that release very limited-production bottlings.

CRISTINA FORNER

It is difficult to be an expatriate. Even if you find business success in your adopted country, you long to return to your homeland. That was certainly the case with Enrique Forner, whose family fled Spain in 1936 at the onset of the Spanish Civil War. He became a successful vintner across the border in France, where he owned two vineyards in the Médoc area of Bordeaux with his brother, Elisée. But he never gave up the dream of re-patriating his family to Spain, including his daughter Cristina, a member of the fourth generation of the Forner family. As the Franco era was waning, Enrique returned to Rioja in 1970 and established Marqués de Cáceres (see page 191) in Cenicero, a village in the Rioja Alta. He was advised in his venture by the famed French oe-nologist Émile Peynaud.

Forner brought back to Rioja some of the viniculture techniques he assimilated during his tenure in France and shared his knowledge with fellow vintners; he became a leader among the vintners in Rioja. For example, Marqués de Cáceres was the first to introduce cold temperature fermentation in stainless steel vats for white wines, now a common practice that results in fresher-tasting whites that appeal to a broad market.

Enrique recruited Cristina in the early 1980s to become export director for the bodega, and today she is president. French in dress and demeanor but Spanish in sangre and spirit, she has built Marqués de Cáceres into the leading Rioja brand in the United States and established distribution in 120 countries worldwide. These accomplishments are nothing short of amazing and have been achieved with classic style, grace, and dedication.

Cristina's legendary father passed away in July 2011. She shares with her father his soft-spoken personality, with more than a hint of a sense of humor, while remaining a confident and intelligent leader. While many houses were busy building additional wineries in and outside of Rioja, Marqués de Cáceres remained steadfast in Cenicero. Cristina is satisfied with her work but quick to mention that "battles are never won, and producing quality wines must be a continual concern." She believes that she brings a female perspective to the business in her ability "to synthesize, listen, filter, and perhaps conform to reachable goals."

MARÍA VARGAS

When you are a native of Haro, the epicenter of centenary wineries, it may seem odd to want to study at Marqués de Murrieta (see page 167), one of few centenary wineries situated outside of town, near Logroño on the border between Rioja Alta and Rioja Baja. But studying at Marqués de Murrieta was María Vargas' goal, and she was accepted. Founded in 1852, it is one of the oldest wineries in Rioja and remains one of the most respected worldwide. María finished her senior thesis in a mere four months in 1995 and was asked to stay on.

A year later Murrieta's owner, Vicente Cebrián Sagarriga Sr., Count of Creixell, died and the massive renovation of the bodega's renowned Ygay estate fell to his son, V. Dalmau Cebrián Sagarriga Jr. María had continued to work in the technical department and describes her first four years at Murrieta as "intoxicating," as if she were under a spell of inspiration that drove her to mastery. During that time, she was offered the job of head winemaker. Honored by the offer but overwhelmed by it, María respectfully declined. Dalmau, with European dignity and the social grace of a true Spanish caballero, respectfully yet firmly replied that he appreciated her honesty but they would try it for a year. She was only twenty-nine when she released her first vintage in 2000.

The two have now worked together for fifteen years, and with their combination of hard work and zeal they have succeeded. María is clearly connected to every inch of the 300 acres (122 hectares) of the Ygay estate. She is passionate that her wines must reflect the origin of her grapes and the essence of her land and Rioja. The two share a vision for how Murrieta should evolve in the twenty-first century to preserve an award-winning history more than 150 years old.

THE RIOJA ALAVESA

Two of the most defining characteristics of the Rioja Alavesa are the contrast of the manicured stone villages and the beauty of the Sierra Cantabria mountain range, which appears to be painted with pastels. Located in this subregion are eighteen municipalities approved by the DOCa for growing grapes, which produce 21 percent of the DOCa wine.

The area, only 115 square miles (300 square kilometers), is easily recognizable, with the mountains majestically to the north and the Ebro to the south. Although protected by the mountains, the region is subject to cold winds and rain from the Atlantic Ocean. Like the rest of DOCa Rioja and especially Rioja Alta, there are great variations in topography, with valleys, slopes, and terraces.

The soil is principally clay and limestone, a dramatic change from the spectrum of colors seen in the soil of nearby Rioja Alta; this clay makes the soil a challenge to work with. Most of the vineyards are on south-facing slopes that gracefully flow down from the Toloño and Cantabria mountain ranges.

Another factor unique to this subregion is the overwhelming prominence of small family properties known as *cosecheros*. These bodegas cite their production in bottles rather than cases.

Only fifteen years ago most wines from the Alavesa were made by carbonic maceration, but today bodegas in the entire Rioja Alavesa subregion are also making aged wines in the Riojan tradition. This use of carbonic maceration is ironic because it was in the Alavesa that barrel aging for young wines began more than a century ago at the great historic Marqués de Riscal winery.

The Alavesa has always been principally Tempranillo country; often notes of balsamic and licorice can be identified as nuances in the wines made with grapes from this subregion. Unlike Rioja Alta and Rioja Baja, Rioja Alavesa has remained an agricultural region without the incursion of industry and manufacturing. Grains are grown at elevations too high for vines, but everywhere else there are vines, and very pampered vines at that. This is a country that has always lived for and from the vine. Ricardo Pérez Villota, a descendant of growers and current partner in the Contino estate, says he made a promise to his father that their vines

RIOJA ALAVESA

to Cantabrian Mountains — to Pyrenees Mountains

N

TOLOÑO MOUNTAINS

Salinillas de Buradón
Briñas
Labastida
Haro
Ebro River
Leza
Samaniego • Laguardia
Labraza
Assa
Elciego
Oyón
Ebro River
Logroño
Najerilla River
Iregua River
Nájera
N-120
0 Miles 5 10
0 Kilometers 10

Jeffrey L. Ward

would be treasured. "We must reflect in our wines what the vine is capable of giving," he says.

In addition to its innovative wines, some of the DOCa's greatest modern architecture can be found in Rioja Alavesa. Not to be missed are Bodegas Ysios, the hotel that is part of the Marqués de Riscal complex, and the functional architecture and spectacular views of Baigorri. We also look forward to the opening of Vega Sicilia in the village of Samaniego.

A ROYAL HELPING HAND

Even in medieval times, the Alavesa was noted for the quality of its wines. The monarchs of Navarre who ruled Álava were progressive for their time and allowed the French and other foreigners as well as Jews to live in the region. They donated many properties to the San Millán monasteries, including the palace of Elciego and the villa at Assa.

It was in 1164 that King Sancho el Sabio (King Sancho the Wise One) ordained that vines should be planted in the region, and this gave rise to the villages of Labastida, Salinillas, and Labraza, which are still significant producers. Within a hundred years, after the reconquest of the region from the Moors, came both federal taxes and taxes on wine.

The wines made in the Alavesa, a province in which Christians, Jews, and Moors coexisted for many centuries, were highly respected. This was validated in 1504 when Queen Isabella la Católica—an extraordinary woman for her time who was forty-one when she finally approved Columbus's plan for exploration—proclaimed that the wines made in the Alavesa should be taxed at a lower rate

CARBONIC MACERATION IN THE RIOJA ALAVESA

Winemakers have many methods for producing wine at their disposal; the most commonly used now worldwide is called the Bordeaux process, in which the grapes are destemmed and then crushed before fermentation. But another method is still used in the Rioja Alavesa more than in the other two Rioja subregions.

Called carbonic maceration or sometimes whole-grape fermentation, the process results in fruity, gentle wines that are ready to drink almost immediately rather than requiring aging. The ultimate use of this method is for the annual release of Beaujolais Nouveau in France, which is uncorked mere weeks after the grapes are picked.

In carbonic maceration whole grapes are fermented in an environment rich in carbon dioxide in a sealed container; most of the juice ferments while it is still inside the grape, which creates the appealing fruity aroma and bright color in the wine.

than the wines from neighboring regions. In her decree she made specific reference to Laguardia. Vine planting surged in the sixteenth century and continued strong until the eighteenth century. Many of the mansions and palaces remaining in Rioja Alavesa are testament to the prosperity created in those centuries.

SALINILLAS DE BURADÓN

This village surrounded with stone walls near Laguardia was founded in 1264 by King Sancho IV of Castile. It was an important frontier point during the reconquest because of its position like a balcony overlooking the Ebro River.

Protected by the Sierra de Toloño mountain range, it is renowned for its salt deposits, after which it was named. The saltwater spring, which is under the walls of the village, was used for salt production until the end of the nineteenth century and now provides the key ingredient for brine at a local cannery.

The most notable feature of the village, which was a stopping point for pilgrims en route to Santiago de Compostela, is the medieval defensive wall. It has two entrances, at the north and south, and was raised and further fortified during the sixteenth and seventeenth centuries to allow sentries to patrol on its top.

The hospital of Santa Ana dates from the fifteenth century, and though the Renaissance palace of the Conde de Oñate on the village square is in ruins, it still provides a glimpse of what must once have been a splendid sight.

THE BASQUE CONNECTION

The Rioja Alavesa is unequivocally more Riojan than it is Basque; in spite of the duality in their regional identity, the people are Riojan in their habits and cuisine. But the interests of the two regions are interwoven like the threads of an old tapestry and cannot be separated. In fact, Haro was the birthplace of Don Diego, the duke who founded the Basque city of Bilbao in 1300.

The growth of the iron industry in the Basque Country during the sixteenth century increased the standard of living and, concomitantly, the Basques' desire to drink the wines of Rioja. The Basques became a large market for Riojan wines, which were transported easily on the excellent system of roads connecting the Alavesa to Basque coastal towns.

The close relationship between the two regions led to prosperity in the seventeenth and eighteenth centuries; this is best reflected in the number of palaces built, such as those around the center square of the village of Labastida. Although Haro was a thriving commercial center, it was eclipsed by Labastida's vineyard growth.

During that time, Basque merchants would come to the market in Haro on Tuesdays to sell everything from fish to iron tools. Because of the challenging soil, many iron tools were custom-crafted to be used in this *campo*. The Basque influence extended as far as Logroño, too: In the seventeenth century a Basque-speaking clerk was hired in the town hall of Logroño to communicate with the drivers bringing goods into the region from the north.

DON FRANCISCO HURTADO DE AMÉZAGA

When you are carried through a winery eight days after your birth and never really considered a career other than winemaking, it is safe to say that it is in your blood. That is surely the case with Don Francisco Hurtado de Amézaga, the current Marqués de Riscal and the great-grandson of the legendary Camilio Hurtado de Amézaga, who founded the bodega of that name (see page 168) in the Rioja Alavesa near the village of Elciego in 1860.

Though titled, Don Francisco is truly Riojan in his total lack of pretension. His nickname is Paco, common enough in Spain, but he's a far cry from the everyday Paco. "Marqués de Riscal is our life. My father was always busy making wine," he said, and his son, Luís, could say the same about him. Luís is now a winemaker at Riscal as well; it is part of their cellular map.

It is not only winemaking but also a close association with the great winemakers of Bordeaux that is a family tradition. Don Francisco's grandfather, who was a diplomat and journalist, hired Jean Pineau, the winemaker at Château Lanessan, as a consultant to the winemakers of Álava in his time. Don Francisco himself hired Émile Peynaud, with whom he had studied enology in the early 1970s. Don Francisco frequently references Peynaud's perspectives on wine, including the great potential for Tempranillo to age in the bottle and how Tempranillo's finesse can be compromised when it is grown in soils outside Rioja. He speaks of the grapes like a grand master, with comfort and ease, reflecting not just decades but centuries of knowledge. When Don Francisco speaks of the Alavesa, the only source of grapes for his red wines, it is with understanding; he demonstrates his care for its soil, vineyards, and indigenous grapes. He believes that the quality and diversity of soil in Rioja is like no other place in the world and cites specific plots as examples of the soil's richness. A total desire for excellence is part of the corporate culture at Riscal. When the management perceived a need to make the bodega a destination for visitors to Spain, the result was not a standard hotel but one designed by the internationally famed architect Frank Gehry, whom Alejandro Aznar, the president of the bodega, met in nearby Bilbao when Gehry was designing the Guggenheim Museum there. The luxury hotel now occupying the center of a complex called the City of Wine was the result of that meeting. For more information on the hotel and its architecture, see page 161.

Don Francisco believes that the building also prompted the bodega to achieve the highest level of excellence. The two could not be more closely integrated. The Gran Reserva wines age in a huge vault directly beneath the hotel's lobby.

THE MEDIEVAL VILLAGE OF LAGUARDIA

Laguardia is one of the most perfectly preserved medieval villages in Spain and is reminiscent of the hilltop towns dotting Tuscany. It was founded in 1164 by King Sancho Abarca as a defensive stronghold for the kingdom of Navarre, and its medieval layout is almost intact. Before the medieval village was built, deep tunnels were carved out of the hill and the village of Laguardia was actually underground.

The tunnels initially were used for defense but over the centuries came to be employed to store wine and eventually even to make wine. In 1486, Laguardia was incorporated into the Kingdom of the Catholic Monarchs (Isabel and Ferdinand), who would unite the kingdoms of Castile and Aragon in 1492 to form what is now Spain, and a new period of construction began. The medieval wall was erected, as were many aristocratic palaces, some restored and still standing.

Laguardia's narrow streets, lined with taverns, restaurants, and shops, converge on the Plaza de San Juan. At either end of the village are the fortified church of San Juan Bautista and that of Santa María de los Reyes, with its exceptional, superbly conserved polychrome portico dating to the seventeenth century. Nearby, you can see the Torre Abacial, an old castle from which the battlements have been removed, which has been refurbished as a bell tower.

But all in Laguardia is not antique. Outside the church of Santa María are two large-scale bronze sculptures. They appear to be tables, one topped with an assortment of handbags and briefcases and the other supporting a collection of shoes and boots for both men and women. The two works pay homage to the leather industry, which remains important in the region.

Laguardia is one of the two DOCa municipalities with extensive planting; it boasts more than 7,500 acres (3,000 hectares) of vineyards. The other village, Alfaro, is in the Rioja Baja.

Aside from its lush vineyards Laguardia is absolutely gorgeous; during the summer there is an abundance of petunias overflowing from balcony windows, and in the early fall there are strings of bright red peppers hanging out to dry to be used for cooking in the colder months. The town has the beauty of a dollhouse with manicured streets and alleys within its walls.

ABOVE: Bronze Sculptures in Laguardia
OPPOSITE: A Laguardia Street
FOLLOWING PAGES: Laguardia in the Autumn

THE RIOJA BAJA

If you leave Logroño and take the highway toward Rioja Baja, you will drive through Rioja Media, which is not a land marked on maps but does form a bridge between subregions. It has the altitude of the adjoining Rioja Alta except for that region's high peaks, and it has the intense sun of areas farther into Rioja Baja which is the easternmost point of the DOCa.

At some point after the Iregua Valley, around the Leza Valley, the highway becomes expansive and you yearn for the freedom that you would have sitting in a convertible with the radio blasting. This region contains a mosaic landscape, with pockets of vineyards, groves of olive and almond trees, ruins, and ancient towns.

Rioja Baja, which means "Lower Rioja," includes land from the adjoining province of Navarre. The subregion contains 37 percent of the DOCa vines. They are planted at altitudes between 980 feet (300 meters) and 2,300 feet (700 meters) in the Yerga Mountains. Rioja Baja also contains the most square miles in Rioja, which is why the soil content varies so widely; most of it is either alluvial (in the river valleys) or rich in iron.

The climate in Rioja Baja, too, is different from that of the other subregions. It gets less rain, and the median temperature is higher. This variation means that the three zones of Rioja can have different quality in their yearly vintages. It is here in the warm Rioja Baja that the harvest begins each year, with vineyards in Alfaro and Aldeanueva in the Jubera, Cidacos, and Alhama valleys leading the way. This region has the typical Mediterranean sun we associate with Spain in the flat valleys, but the high elevations and mountains are some of Rioja Baja's best-kept secrets.

CALAHORRA

The Cidacos River passes through this town of 23,000—second in size only to Logroño—on its trip north to join the Ebro. The history of this village dates back more than 2,000 years; it was named Calagurris by its original Celtiberian inhabitants, and the town is famous for its four years of fighting the Roman general Pompey between 76 BCE and 72 BCE. The Romans later called it Calagurris Nassica to distinguish it from other nearby

OPPOSITE: The Cathedral of San Francisco in Calahorra

towns. It was one of the most important cities on the Iberian Peninsula to fall under Moorish control, but it was retaken by the Christians in 1054.

Legend states that the Jews established themselves in Calahorra in the sixth century BCE, and it became the largest Jewish community in Rioja; Calahorra is now listed as part of the Camino del Sefarad, a string of Jewish sites scattered throughout Spain. The Cathedral of San Francisco, completed in 1484, is monumental, and its museum contains the Thora, a collection of Jewish prayers written on goatskin and rolled on a wooden stick that are conserved here to honor the Hebrew community.

Calahorra was the birthplace in 1093 of Rabbi Abraham Ibn Ezra, a distinguished writer and man of letters during the Middle Ages. For the first part of his life he was a poet, and his literary legacy consists of short and extremely popular handbooks in a wide variety of fields, including grammar and poetics, astrology and arithmetic, and astronomy and religious speculations, as well as both short and lengthy biblical commentaries. The Jewish community flourished in Calahorra until the Edict of Expulsion in 1492.

That year also began the exploration of the New World, called the American Adventure. Between 1492 and 1599 more than 450 Riojans, 5 percent of them women, participated. Perhaps the most famous is Martín de Calahorra, the only Riojan who floated his own ship to the Americas. He benefited from a good education as well as a privileged position in society. Together with a local judge, Alonzo de Zuazo, he departed for the New World in April 1517. Among his peers he was highly respected and revered. In 1519 he learned of the infamous expedition of Hernán Cortés and his conquests in Mexico and headed to the Yucatán. Thereafter he settled in Mexico and had seven children.

THE DAWNING OF A NEW ERA

Rioja Baja is the subregion to watch and experience, whether it is through the wineries and wines or on a visit; it is experiencing its coming-out party. Without a doubt, it is the area undergoing the greatest growth, with new bodegas opening each year.

Many Rioja Bajans believe the agricultural spirit here and the history of cultivation of various products make them more adaptable than those in other areas of Rioja; that adaptability has given them greater creativity in process and cultivation. Generations of growers who used to cultivate asparagus and the other vegetables typical of this area have abandoned those crops to concentrate on the vine.

There is increased professionalism among the growers and bold winemakers. Rioja Baja natives and trailblazers such as Gabriel Pérez of Bodegas Ontañón, Amador Escudero of Valsacro, and Álvaro Palacios of Palacios Remondo may differ in demeanor and generation but concur in having a Rioja Bajan spirit. This is based on enormous reverence for their land, respect for the heritage of their ancestors, and a commitment to carry it forward.

These winemakers do not pretend to make Rioja Alta or Alavesa wines in their subregion; fruit ripens differently here and produces a richer style of wine that is typical of this region alone. Historically these lands were planted mostly with Garnacha, which vintners from other regions would buy for blending. Today, however, as in all of the DOCa Rioja, Tempranillo dominates the vineyards, with a mere scattering of Graciano and Garnacha. The remaining Garnacha vines are very old and prized, and the move toward Tempranillo here is controversial: some watchers of this shift, both within and outside the region, wish that Rioja Baja would encourage more Garnacha production in the coming years.

ÁLVARO PALACIOS

Although Álvaro Palacios also makes wine in two other Spanish DO regions, he is a purebred Riojan and an Alfareño through and through. Alfaro is a town at the eastern end of the Rioja Baja, a luminous part of the region that is warmed by the sun.

I first met Alvaro at the Vinexpo wine fair in Bordeaux in 1987 where, at the time, many in the wine world jested and jeered at his prediction that he would make a $75 bottle of Spanish wine in Priorat, then a small region no one had heard of or could pronounce. But he did succeed. After his schooling, he focused his winemaking efforts in Priorat and Bierzo during the 1990s. Álvaro has always had a twinkle in his eye, and now droplets of glittering wisdom augment the light he radiates.

Álvaro returned to Rioja Baja to take over Bodegas Palacios Remondo after the death of his father in 2000; he and his brother, Rafael, have made the bodega one of the rising stars of Rioja. He now makes La Montesa, a Crianza blend of Tempranillo and Garnacha, with grapes grown in south-facing vineyards at an altitude of almost 2,000 feet (550 meters) on the lower slopes of the Yerga Mountains. His father planted the vineyard in 1989, the same year Álvaro left to study in Bordeaux; he also traveled extensively in Australia and California to gain a broad perspective on winemaking. Unlike those of many of his neighbors, his wines are aged only in French oak rather than American. He also makes a white wine; Placet is made from 100 percent Viura and is fermented in oval French oak barrels.

Álvaro has great affection for his vineyards and a relationship with the vines and soil. That is where his passion lies. His great joy comes from growing old vines and maximizing their ability and expression. He holds a cupped hand to his forehead like a Mediterranean sculpture and emphasizes "logic" as his goal. It is the logic of the land that defines his decisions as a winemaker.

GABRIEL PÉREZ MARZO
AND BODEGAS ONTAÑÓN

For three generations Gabriel Pérez Marzo's family grew grapes in the small village of Quel in the Rioja Baja; each year they would sell them to bodegas in Rioja Alta that, depending on the year, would come to buy grapes with a lesser or greater sense of urgency.

It was around 1980 that Gabriel decided that this practice of serving as a source of grapes but not a source of wine had to end; as a grower in the Rioja Baja he no longer would be beholden to those in the other subregions. He began a consistent pace of purchasing land, and the first wines from Bodegas Ontañón (see page 193) were released in 1985. Today he believes that in ten years some of the greatest wines of the DOCa Rioja will come from the Baja. He states with Buddha-like wisdom that "progress compensates for lost time."

His mantra certainly lives on in his daughter, Raquel, who moves with supersonic speed, passion, and intelligence. Together with her confident and reflective winemaker brother, Rubén, she cultivates a whopping 620 acres (250 hectares) of prized vineyards in the Cidacos and Alhama valleys, with 30 percent of their vines planted at an altitude of at least 1,640 feet (500 meters). Raquel and Rubén live their legacy anything but lightly. They exemplify the new generation of Rioja Bajans who are truly making history.

TEMPRANILLO
AND
HER SISTERS

4

Each of the great wine regions of the world is associated primarily with one grape—a grape that finds its finest expression in the climate and soil of a particular place. When wine drinkers think of a red wine from Burgundy, they are thinking of Pinot Noir; for Bordeaux, it is Cabernet Sauvignon; and for Barolo, it is Nebbiolo.

In Rioja, Tempranillo (tem-pra-**knee**-yoh) reigns as queen. Although Tempranillo has been planted around the world at an accelerated rate in recent decades, the Tempranillo of Rioja is singular. This Tempranillo expresses the nobility of the grape in a way that is not found in any other wine region, and it is nobility that produces a wine of tremendous elegance.

Tempranillo's domination of the vineyard lands of Rioja is a fairly recent phenomenon, especially in the context of the more than eleven centuries of grape cultivation in the region. But in the spirit of twenty-first century Rioja, with bold modern architecture juxtaposed with centuries-old buildings and chefs producing drinkable shot-glass versions of patatas (potatoes) a la Riojana, the virtues of this new protagonist should be explored; thus, much of this chapter is devoted to this one grape. At the beginning of the twentieth century about forty-five grape varieties were cultivated in Rioja; by 1942 about seventeen of those remained. The diversity of grapes, however, is reflected more on paper than in reality. In fact, seven varieties—four red and three white—account for more than 99 percent of Rioja's vines. But Tempranillo today inhabits about 80 percent of the vineyards; the other six varieties share the remaining land. This means the harvest of Tempranillo takes place on 190 square miles (49,000 hectares).

In 1973, Garnacha accounted for 39 percent of the grapes in Rioja, with Tempranillo lagging behind at 31 percent. A decade later, plantings of Tempranillo had increased to 40 percent. Plantings dramatically increased in the 1990s, when all three subzones of the DOCa Rioja shifted vine space to Tempranillo. This resulted from a growing awareness of Tempranillo's potential and what can be extracted from this grape. As a grape variety, Tempranillo demonstrates tremendous versatility; wines made from it can be enjoyed right away, but they reach their greatest expression with aging. In addition, Tempranillo adapts well to different soils and produces wines of great balance. It is a medium-bodied grape with great red fruit aromatics.

CHAPTER OPENER: **Badarán Vineyard**
PREVIOUS PAGES: **Huércanos Vineyard**
PREVIOUS RIGHT TOP: **Viura Grapes**
PREVIOUS RIGHT BOTTOM: **Tempranillo Grapes**
LEFT: **Flowering Tempranillo**

TEMPRANILLO'S VINEYARD LIFE

Before the sensuality of wine in a glass, there is the anticipatory pleasure of seeing the grapes growing in the vineyard. Tempranillo is a small bluish-black grape with large, long cylindrical bunches. It is thick-skinned, but unlike other thick-skinned grapes, it does not take well to drought or excessive heat or rain; it is a perfect fit, therefore, with the climate of Rioja. It is this climate—with its cool mountain air and cool nights—and the unique terroir of Rioja that define Tempranillo.

Temprano means "early" in Spanish, and Tempranillo is an early harvest grape as a result of its short vegetation cycle of 215 days. The cycle begins with budding in mid-April, followed by flowering two months later. Tempranillo customarily is harvested in early to middle October, one to two weeks before the rest of the region's varieties. The exact time for harvest varies from location to location in the region, depending mostly on altitude.

Tempranillo's technical properties present both blessings and challenges for a winemaker. The grape is prone to diseases and is high in acidity. But Riojan winemakers have a relationship with Tempranillo and find it a forgiving grape. It is very fertile at the flowering stage, producing myriad buds. In this respect Tempranillo is a marked contrast to Garnacha, which aborts frequently at the flowering stage.

Tempranillo has become so well liked that winemakers all over the world have been inspired to plant it in their countries, although it does not really travel well. Acres of Tempranillo can be found throughout many DO regions of Spain, on various continents, in countries such as Argentina and Australia, and in more than fifteen wine-producing states in the United States.

In Rioja, Tempranillo has established its root system and its relationship with the soil. Rioja and Tempranillo have evolved together with wisdom; they work together like the fit of a cherished baseball glove or a pair of well-worn dancing shoes. As the famed Spanish wine writer José Peñín commented recently, "Tempranillo is perfect in Rioja due to three key factors; it needs cold, sun, and heat. Tempranillos of Rioja have elegance and finesse."

Regardless of whether the wine is made to be consumed young, slightly aged, or highly aged, Tempranillo harnesses its potential to produce quality wines that are considered elegant and work harmoniously with the other essential components of a world-class wine. Tempranillo is the raw material needed to create a great "food wine." These wines balance alcohol content, color, and acidity with soft tannins and fruit. It is *quality* and *elegance* that unite all wines made with Tempranillo of Rioja.

VOICE OF THE VINTNERS

Tempranillo, like all great wine grapes in the world, has a personality. This personality is revealed especially keenly to those who work with the grape—the growers, vineyard agronomists, and winemakers that know it best. Here is a sampling of their thoughts:

"Violets are the best descriptor of Tempranillo's floral components—which then move into red fruits such as strawberries and plums."

— Jesús Madrazo, Contino

"Tempranillo still has not reached her full potential here in Rioja, but this will happen soon."

— Luis Lucendo, Bodegas El Coto

"Tempranillo is singularity, typical of our land, from which it takes its nuances, flavors, and aromas. It bears on its cluster the effort of an entire region and its people dedicated to wine. There is elegance in its complexity, its structure, its harmony, which has given us experience and maturity."

— Rubén Pérez Cuevas, Bodegas Ontañón

"Tempranillo in Rioja is balanced; she reaches a great level of harmony with other components of the wine."

— Gonzalo Rodríguez, Barón de Ley

"Tempranillo's strengths are her aromatics. The nose of Tempranillo opens up completely like a decorative fan."

— Elena Adell, Bodegas Campo Viejo

"Tempranillo of Rioja is capable of producing one of the most elegant wines in the world and has the desirable combination of elegance and potency."

— María José López de Heredia, Viña Tondonia

"Color, aroma, and the flavors of red fruits and licorice are her best virtues."

— Óscar Tobía, Bodegas Tobía

"Tempranillo in the vineyard expresses the characteristics of the soil . . . we can achieve a mature wine with the aromas of rose, red and black fruits, with round tannins that are powerful but never green or astringent."

— Juan Cañas, Luis Cañas

"Tempranillo is like a loyal, good friend in our family. She is a noble and elegant grape."

— Roberto Ijalba, Bodegas Santalba

"Tempranillo is one of the greatest varieties in the world. It is honest, it lets you experiment, it's grateful. If you capture her right she has it all—aromatics and tannins, and best of all, she is accepting of blending with other varieties, like having a roommate."

— María Vargas, Marqués de Murrieta

"With low yields Tempranillo shines like a star. Tempranillo does not travel well. Tempranillo reaches its height through aging."

— Álvaro Palacios, Bodegas Palacios Remondo

"Tempranillo is the soul of the land of Rioja. She is elegant and sensual with a high character that will leave an indelible mark."

— Miguel Ángel Muro, Bodegas Miguel Ángel Muro

"Tempranillo is like a beautiful, fit woman who does not need too much makeup. When she walks by, everyone appreciates her beauty. This feminine perspective is Tempranillo; she is our star variety and is both subtle and elegant."

— Rafael Vivanco, Dinastía Vivanco

"Elegance. Tempranillo of Rioja is a very kind, approachable variety and produces wines that are easy to drink."

— Jesús Martínez Bujanda, Bodegas Valdemar

"Tempranillo is indigenous to Rioja, and it shows. She is like great jazz; she's not classical nor is she rock 'n' roll. She's in between."

— Carlos Estecha, Bodegas Federico Paternina

"Tempranillo is the grape variety that best takes advantage of the climate of the Rioja region to produce high-quality grapes."
— Emilio Sojo Nalda, Bodegas Riojanas

"Tempranillo is elegant; she is the complete package. She is aromatic, soft yet with complex tannins, and she is as round and attractive in aroma as she is on the palate."
— María Barua González, Bodegas LAN

"In Toro, Tempranillo is very high in alcohol, and in Ribera del Duero Tempranillo is very structured and rustic. But in Rioja, Tempranillo is refined; there is power, structure, and elegance all in balance."
— Fernando Remírez de Ganuza,
Bodegas Remírez de Ganuza

"To talk about Tempranillo of Sonsierra means to be seduced by her structure, harmony, freshness, and elegance. On this outstanding and unique soil, as a variety she is perfectly adapted to the climatology profoundly shaped by the Sierra de Cantabria mountain range."
— Marcos Eguren, Bodegas Eguren

"Tempranillo from Rioja has a unique character reflecting all the authenticity of the land where she was born and where she is happiest: La Rioja."
— Guillermo de Aranzabal, La Rioja Alta

"Tempranillo gives us versatility in viniculture and viticulture. Tempranillo is 80 percent handling and 20 percent variety, whereas Cabernet Sauvignon is completely the reverse. You can obtain different results from Tempranillo cultivated in the same plot."
— César Castro, Bodegas y Viñedos Castillo Labastida

"She is exquisitely scented with a complex and delicate perfume that contains floral notes, earth, fruits, and spices all blended into a bewitching fragrance. Her character gives the impression of being rude, but as time passes she demonstrates elegance."
— Luís Zalaba, Bodegas Marqués de Vitoria

"Tempranillo is a perfect master of ceremonies as she makes room for those with which she cohabitates, like Garnacha, Mazuelo, and Graciano. She becomes more complete with them, which only augments her greatness."
— Pilar Bello, Bodegas Bretón

"If I have to define Tempranillo in a word, it's elegance. In two words it's elegance and complexity. Other varieties are better suited to making wines of impact; this one makes complex wines."
— Luis Valentín, Valenciso

"Tempranillo is the soul of our wines. I like to highlight its distinctive aroma and subtle licorice, and velvety mouth feel."
— Iván Ausejo, Antiguas Viñas de Rioja.

"Tempranillo lives in the many hills and ridges of our land, exposed to all the winds but stroked by the Ebro River. She is a great ambassador for our people due to her elegance, her freshness, and her guarantee of long aging ability."
— Agustín Santolaya, Bodegas RODA

"I would introduce Tempranillo of Rioja as a shy person who does not speak loudly, but with time you realize that she is much more interesting than what you imagined."
— Telmo Rodríguez, Nuestra Señora de Remelluri

"I love Tempranillo as a variety because it is so versatile. You can make everything with it —young wine, avant-garde wines, and reserva wines."
— Juan B. Chávarri, Bodega La Grajera, a research facility run by La Rioja's Department of Agriculture (CIDA)

"Tempranillo shows all its potential in poor soils, balanced vines, and cool climates. It brings personality, elegance, and kindness to our wines."
— Diego Pinilla, Bodegas Bilbaínas

MARÍA MARTÍNEZ SIERRA

Long before her contemporaries, this Riojan fireball who speaks with conviction, passion, and a pointed finger became a staunch advocate of Tempranillo in general and the Tempranillo of Rioja in particular. Now the chief winemaker at Bodegas Montecillo (see page 170) in Fuenmayor in the heart of Rioja Alta, she released her first wine for Christmas in 1978.

Don Laureano Santaolalla Azpilicueta, a close family friend who was part of a well-known Riojan wine family, first influenced her career; he would dance jotas Riojanas (traditional folk dances) with her grandfather. He took an interest in young María; he appreciated her studious, strong character and believed in her potential.

On a bright and sunny spring day in March 1968, Don Laureano took María and a shovel into his manicured gardens and began to dig furiously without sharing the reason for the excursion. What was revealed thirty minutes and 3 feet (slightly less than 1 meter) later were buried bottles of wine composed of 100 percent Tempranillo.

Don Laureano told the young María that Tempranillo was the greatest indigenous grape of Spain and she should not forget that. Her skin had goose bumps, and she remembers that moment well. They proceeded to uncork the bottles Don Laureano had buried as a young man and found that many were just fantastic; they still held marvelous fruit and tannins. This experience was enough to move María to commit totally to Tempranillo and become its ambassador in other countries years before many of her peers. Back in the 1980s people would ask her to repeat the name of this unknown grape variety. "Tempa . . . Tempra . . . Tempra—what did you say?" she recalls them asking.

By committing to Tempranillo she helped establish Montecillo as we know it today, a respected bodega and producer of monovarietal (single-grape) Riojan Tempranillos. Her view is that women approach winemaking differently from their male colleagues. Believing that wine is a living thing, she perceives that a female winemaker brings feeling and sensuality to her bodega; that is expressed in the wines.

TEMPRANILLO'S RED SISTERS

It is in the blending of grape varieties that the true art of the winemaker emerges. In Rioja, Tempranillo often is blended with other red grape varieties, two of which have been saved from near extinction. Rioja's rescued varieties and the pioneers who navigated these waters to save them help define the personality of Rioja today with conviction.

GARNACHA TINTA

Garnacha Tinta (ghar-**nah**-sha **teen**-tah) is best known by its French name, Grenache, and is extremely popular the world over. In the past, this indigenous grape dominated plantings in Rioja: in 1900 Garnacha accounted for 54 square miles (14,000 hectares) of land there, but its popularity decreased during the latter part of the twentieth century and into the twenty-first.

Twenty-five years ago almost 40 percent of vines in DOCa Rioja consisted of Garnacha, but with the recent supremacy of Tempranillo, that amount is now about 9 percent, or 23 square miles (6,000 hectares). Historically it thrived in the Rioja Baja, as it does today, but now more than 65 percent of the Garnacha vines are planted in Rioja Alta. Some of the most historic villages for great Garnacha vines in the Rioja Baja are Tudelilla, El Redal, and the Yerga Mountain slopes in Alfaro.

Part of the enduring reverence for Garnacha is due to its hearty temperament. In a vineyard in Rioja Baja that has not seen rain for more than two months, drought is evident in the Tempranillo and Graciano vines but not the Garnacha. The Garnacha's leaves appear healthy, and the grapes are corpulent and ripe. Some winemakers believe that in Rioja Alta the Garnacha does not mature well some years because of lack of heat.

The blending of a small percentage of juicy Garnacha into the more austere Tempranillo produces wines of great richness with floral and fresh fruit aromas. The Garnacha also enhances the color, body, and alcohol of the primarily Tempranillo wines.

In earlier eras, when Garnacha accounted for a larger percentage of Rioja's vineyards, it was used to make rosé wines that were 100 percent Garnacha. Unfortunately, the reduced planting has largely removed these wines from the market, which is a shame because they are so delicious. Today in Rioja, Garnacha is used primarily as a small blending element in Tempranillo-based red wines.

JORGE MUGA

The limbs of the Muga family tree in the small Riojan villages of Gimileo and Villalba de Rioja extend back more than five hundred years in one genealogical chart alone. The family knows they've been there longer, but earlier records were lost in a fire. Thus, it is very safe to say that the Muga family has cultivated vineyards in Rioja Alta, very close to Haro, as governments have risen and fallen and centuries have come and gone.

The 1920s were challenging years in Rioja Alta. Although the plague of phylloxera had been eradicated, grape growers like the Mugas were at the mercy of established bodegas to purchase their grapes. They courageously decided to start their own bodega and begin bottling their own wines during hard times.

The Bodegas Muga we know today (see page 170), with a winery in Haro, is now three generations old.

It was winemaker Jorge Muga's grandparents, Issac Muga Sr. and his wife, Aurora Caño, who founded the winery in 1932. Aurora was also from a winemaking family; her father, Jorge Caño, was the manager of the great historic bodega La Rioja Alta.

The original building they purchased was in disrepair and collapsed in the 1960s. By then the bodega was successful, so they hired a master carpenter, Jesús Azcarate—a native of the nearby village of San Vicente de la Sonsierra—to renovate the structure they purchased to replace the old building. He also built the oak fermentation vats still in use today. From this initial relationship, Azcarate became the Mugas' in-house cooper.

Jorge is the son of Issac Muga Jr., and his first cousin, Juan Muga, is the son of

Issac's brother, Manuel. While Jorge works at the winery, Juan tirelessly travels the world to represent their wines and family legacy. This is clearly a bodega run on the "theme of team." They share the spirit of pride in their name and the quality of their wines, and they jointly apply a diligent ethic of hard work. However, equally, they experience the rich joy that generosity and sharing in tradition, fun, family, and friends gives us all.

At first glance Jorge appears to be a quiet man of reserve. But once you get to know him you realize that great intellect and humor coexist harmoniously in his soul. He studied agronomic engineering at the University of Pamplona at a time when enology did not exist as a major, and he then pursued advanced degrees in viticulture and conducted soil research studies.

From his earliest recollections Jorge has had a constant love for nature; today he enjoys mushroom foraging, fishing, and hunting. He also recalls his adoration for the vineyards as a child and says it was as if the "vineyards lived in their home." He remembers being fascinated by the different behavior of vines sharing the same plot. That is what makes a winemaker. His relationship with the vines is innate, not acquired.

GRACIANO

Although it represents only 2 percent of grape cultivation today, a mere 3 square miles (830 hectares), the wine-makers of Rioja are seduced by Graciano (grah-see-**ah**-noh). They smile and wiggle when they talk about it as a model variety.

This prized grape variety was on the verge of extinction in the late twentieth century. We can be thankful to a few winemakers in the new generation who continued to use it and assured its future as a grape to blend with Tempranillo in DOCa Rioja wines. *Gracia* means "grace" in Spanish, and winemakers believe that grace and style are what this grape adds to wine.

Graciano is believed to have originated from some of the oldest vineyards in Rioja, principally in Rioja Alta and Rioja Alavesa. However, in this century, some of the best results with Graciano are coming from Rioja Baja. Many winemakers believe that the vines planted in the Iregua Valley yield the best results.

Wines that are 100 percent Graciano are rare, and they can be spectacular, with an intense color. The aromas can be strong and are unique, reminiscent of star fruit, green pepper, and spice. In recent vintages, only in 2001, 2005, 2007, and 2009 have 100 percent Graciano wines been made.

Graciano is a finicky grape to grow, requiring heat and humidity as well as clay soils. It also needs hydration and cannot handle stress well. Ripening late in the harvest cycle, Graciano produces small grapes with a tough black skin. Graciano wine has good acidity and tannins that lend themselves well to wines destined for aging. Despite its finicky nature and challenges, the wines it yields have great allure.

MAZUELO

Mazuelo (mah-zoo-**eh**-loh) accounts for 3 percent of the vines in Rioja. It is a grape variety of Spanish origin, and some theories state that the name originates from the Basque word for grape mats. Like Graciano, Mazuelo is blended in small quantities with Tempranillo when wine is destined for aging as a Reserva or Gran Reserva.

Most winemakers cite acidity as the reason to include Mazuelo in wines, along with color and tannins. Mazuelo is not known for its aroma, although some winemakers believe that fruit from old vines adds sumptuous black plum or vegetal overtones to the wine. However, Mazuelo vines are low yielding and very susceptible to oïdium, a powdery mildew—two explanations for its scarcity in Rioja.

OPPOSITE: Garnacha Blanca

RIOJA'S WHITE GRAPES

Rioja is synonymous with red wine in the same way that one automatically thinks of Bordeaux or Barolo wines being red. But Tempranillo's white relatives are not forgotten stepsisters in the region.

VIURA

Known as Macabeo in other parts of Spain as well as in vineyards around the world, Viura (vee-**your**-rah) accounts for 7 percent of Rioja's vines, the largest amount for any white grape. Its large and hefty bunches of grapes announce its presence in the vineyards. Viura contributes acidity and structure to wines, and barrel fermentation seems to extract complexity from the grape. In a process now illegal, traditionally winemakers would add 5 percent Viura to their Gran Reservas to punch up the acidity. Producers today make white Rioja with 100 percent Viura, and the style is usually austere and structured.

MALVASÍA

Also found in Portugal and Italy, Malvasía (mal-vah-**see**-yah) is planted on less than 200 acres (76 hectares) in Rioja; it is a grape that has rarely left the Mediterranean region. The fruit is sensitive to rot, but the grape is being planted more often in Rioja despite its problems. Malvasía is an aromatic grape with low acidity, which makes it a good partner to blend with Viura.

GARNACHA BLANCA

The white mutation of Garnacha Tinta is planted on only 37 acres (15 hectares) in Rioja and is cultivated only in the cool zones. Garnacha Blanca (ghar-**nah**-sha **blahnk**-ah) adds good acidity to blends and a combination of citrus and apple aromas.

ORGANZA

One of the few wines on the market composed of all three of Rioja's prominent white grapes is Sierra Cantabria Organza Rioja Blanco. A testament to winemaker Marcos Eguren's innovation, it is made from late-harvest fruit fermented at low temperatures with some oak aging.

RIOJA 2008
DENOMINACIÓN DE ORIGEN CALIFICADA
ORGANZA
SIERRA CANTABRIA

NEWLY APPROVED GRAPE VARIETIES

Discipline is a good thing. It helps in keeping intentions clear. The Rioja Regulatory Control Board has remained steadfast in the discipline it exerts over the grape varieties permitted in wine sold as DOCa Rioja. Although there have been protests and queries, the control board has remained firm.

During the last few decades, the rules have been loosened to allow a few experimental foreign grapes to be planted at the urging of some growers and winemakers.

However, it was the group that was pushing for those grapes that was the first to abandon them. To quote Gonzalo Rodríguez, winemaker at Barón de Ley, "fashionable varieties are usually the ones that are easiest to manage; Syrah, for example, you can grow it anywhere." But grapes such as Tempranillo in Rioja push the skills of winemakers; it takes a winemaker of substance to work with complicated grapes and still deliver a sumptuous outcome.

By 2009, however, four *indigenous* grape varieties, one red and three white, were approved by the control board. These four sisters—all rescued from extinction— had been studied in several research projects. They are now being cultivated in Rioja in minuscule amounts, but the movement is exciting.

MATURANA TINTA

This is a unique red grape that is not cultivated anywhere else in the world. It has great potential to fulfill the definition that Riojans are working so hard to preserve. It demonstrates their commitment to their heritage.

Unlike other varieties cultivated in Rioja, wine from Maturana Tinta (mah-tur-**ah**-na **teen**-tah) has a deep purple tone and is opaque. Although some winemakers use descriptions such as balsamic vinegar and green pepper to characterize this wine, others find the aromas akin to Middle Eastern spices with overtones of chocolate. It retains, however, the signature soft tannins for which Rioja wines are known. The extant vineyards are in Navarette, a village not far from Logroño that is also known for pottery.

MATURANA BLANCA

It is up to Rioja to keep Maturana Blanca (mah-tur-**ah**-na **blahnk**-ah) alive; it is not cultivated anywhere else in the world. This grape is not a mutation of Maturana Tinta but a variety all to itself. Though its susceptibility to botrytis rot works against cultivation, its aromas and flavors of apples, bananas, and citrus are qualities welcomed by winemakers.

TEMPRANILLO BLANCO

This white mutation of the queen of Rioja grapes is still cultivated only in Rioja. It was first identified in 1988; the white grapes were found on a branch of a red Tempranillo vine in the village of Murillo de Rio Leza in the Leza Valley. White Tempranillo's molecular markers confirm a 98 percent similarity to red Tempranillo, but the color and exotic white grape aromas mark this as its own variety. The grape asserts an intense aroma of banana, citrus, and tropical fruits; has an intense roundness on the palate; and adapts well to barrel fermentation.

TURRUNTÉS

Similar to both Tempranillo Blanco and Maturana Blanca, Turruntés (tur-run-**tes**) should not be confused with Torrontés, a white grape cultivated in both Galicia and Argentina. This grape is noted for its apple aroma as well as vegetal, almost herbaceous qualities. The approval of this grape variety could add a new dimension of distinction to white Riojas in the future.

JESÚS MARTÍNEZ BUJANDA

More than twenty years ago, Jesús Martínez Bujanda was a man doing things ahead of time—like a character from *Star Trek*, he was operating in another galaxy. He is a pioneer in the formation of Bodegas Inspiración, part of Bodegas Valdemar (see page 175) in Rioja Alavesa. He was the first winemaker and remains one of the few to produce wines made from 100 percent Tempranillo Blanco. This represents a natural progression of his work spanning four decades.

The fifth generation of his family in the wine business and a winemaker for more than forty years, Jesús understands grapes and wine intuitively—almost viscerally. He talks about the vines as if they were members of the family and describes how his father saw life through the prism of the vine.

Decades ago when his contemporaries rarely visited the bodegas next door, Jesús spent six weeks in Napa talking with vintners and experiencing different grapes. It was after that visit that Jesús became a staunch proponent of planting Cabernet Sauvignon. He eventually changed his mind and became disillusioned with its limitations in Rioja. Instead, he has opted to devote his work to indigenous grapes such as Graciano, Maturana Tinta, and, most recently, Tempranillo Blanco.

His work with Tempranillo Blanco began fifteen years ago with his experimentation with clones and different subzones and plots. He also conducted a stimulating and formative research exchange with Juan Bautista Chávarri of La Grajera, a research bodega of the CIDA (Centro de Investigación y Desarrollo Agroalimentario), owned by La Rioja's Department of Agriculture.

The name of Bodega Inspiración, of course, means "inspiration" in Spanish, and it reflects the spirit of honoring the regional distinctions of Rioja's indigenous grape while maximizing innovation. Bodega Inspiración represents the dynamic that is alive in Rioja today. The work of rescuing and experimenting with indigenous grape varieties is sustained by passion, not commercial viability. It is this sense of pride and building upon the region's heritage that exemplifies twenty-first-century Rioja.

CATEGORIES, STYLES, AND REGULATION

Wines around the world can be divided into two groups: those whose strengths are derived from potency and those which exude elegance. Elegance is what we taste when we drink the wines of Rioja.

Winemaking in Rioja goes back more than 1,200 years, but the wines we drink today reflect the evolution of this art form into the late twentieth and early twenty-first centuries. What is derived from the past is the pride of winemakers whose heritage goes back centuries on the same small vineyards, since land in Rioja is still widely distributed rather than concentrated in a few large parcels. They produce wines united by elegance derived from the Tempranillo grape that dominates today's vineyards, but with diversity within every style and price range. They juxtapose twenty-first-century tools and vision with the traditions of the past.

The Tempranillo of Rioja creates wines with a balance of red fruit, acidity, and soft tannins. They are accessible to the palate and are excellent wines for food pairing. Many Riojas can also stand alone, however, as a bar wine or at a cocktail party.

Part of the heritage of Rioja is the strict regulation of the wines by the Rioja Regulatory Control Board (see page 145), which has a deep concern for quality control that dates back centuries.

AGING CATEGORIES

Wines bottled under the auspices of the DOCa Rioja are categorized by the length of time they are aged. All wines start the aging process in 60-gallon (225-liter) oak casks and then are bottled for further aging. Within each age category of wine there is stylistic variation that depends on the producer, the vintage, the vineyards, and the percentage of other grape varieties blended with the Tempranillo. Certain conclusions can be drawn about the wine from its color-coded guarantee of origin label alone because of the regulations set forth and overseen by the Rioja Regulatory Control Board. This is a small guarantee of origin and age category label that is found on the back of the bottle, and it is an easy way to tell quickly what aging a wine has undergone.

COSECHA

The olive green age label identifies the youngest of the categories, which is aged for less than one year in oak and less than one year in the bottle before release. *Cosecha* (ko-**say**-sha) means "harvest" or "vintage" in Spanish, and these wines are the youngest of the group. Cosecha wines sometimes are called *joven* (young), but this term

CHAPTER OPENER: Traditional Bottle Room at an Eguren Family Winery
PREVIOUS PAGES: The Jubera Valley
PREVIOUS TOP RIGHT: Bottling Wine
PREVIOUS BOTTOM RIGHT: Aging Barrels at Labastida

130

rarely appears on a wine label. Cosechas are meant to be consumed within about two years of the vintage date; they are generally quality fruity, simple wines.

Many Cosecha wines reflect most modern styles of Rioja such as high expression (see page 144), Vinos de Autor, and New Wave. Unlike standard Cosechas, these wines are highly complex and powerful and may be aged for years.

CRIANZA

Any red Crianza wine, identified by a bright red age label, is at least two years old before it is released from the winery; it must age for at least one year in oak. *Crianza* (cree-**ahn**-zah) is translated as "breeding," and these wines are bred to deliver satisfaction. In this world of increasingly globalized wines that are released immediately to market, ready to drink, Crianza wines offer aging, value, and pleasure. They are made, however, to be at their peak four years after harvest, so cellaring them for just a short period will produce wonderful results. Even at the time of release from the winery they have some age on them, which adds dimension and complexity to the wine.

If you should find a bottle of Crianza that is years or even decades old, do not assume it has turned to vinegar. Recently, some twenty-year-old bottles of Crianza were drinking wonderfully, with mature fruit and acidity. They served as testament to the ability of Tempranillo to age gracefully.

White and rosé Crianza wines spend six months in oak and before release.

RESERVA

Reserva (ray-**zerv**-ah) wines, identified by their burgundy age label, often are sought for their high quality-to-price ratio, the equation that defines value. Reservas must be aged in oak casks for a full year and then spend two years in the bottle before release from the winery. This slightly mutes the fruit flavors of the wine and introduces a note of earthiness while allowing the different flavor and texture elements to knit together and become more complex.

Singular to Rioja and steeped in tradition, Reservas (and Gran Reservas; see page 132) receive respectful care and consideration. They are produced only in select years, and the wines are created from carefully chosen vineyards from the 144 municipalities in the DOCa Rioja; the choices are based on both the fruit's quality and its aging potential.

Reservas can be enjoyed when you purchase them or cellared for an average of five to ten years. Because of the small quantities produced, if you find one you especially enjoy, it is best to purchase more while the opportunity still exists.

White and rosé Reservas spend at least six months in oak casks and then eighteen months in the bottle before release.

GRAN RESERVA

Gran Reserva (grahn ray-**zerv**-ah) wines are marked with a royal blue age label to assert their position as the royalty of Rioja wines; they represent a great tradition of cellaring wines in the bodega where they were produced. Gran Reservas must be aged two years in oak casks and three years in the bottle before their release from the winery; many are held at the bodega even longer.

Although they can be enjoyed right away, Gran Reservas benefit from up to fifteen to twenty years of additional aging, although older ones can shine too, like great old Bordeaux. There are sometimes very few bottles released in this category in certain vintages or by certain wineries. These are wines you will not regret purchasing, and they will perform well in the future, gaining more earth and even mushroom aromas as they develop.

Gran Reserva white wines are not common. They must spend at least four years at the bodega before release, one year of that time in oak casks.

JESÚS MADRAZO

Like many vintners in Rioja, Jesús Madrazo was born into the business. His father, Don José Madrazo, was the viticulturalist who worked hand in glove with the legendary Basilio Izquierdo, who was head winemaker at C.V.N.E. and Contino for more than thirty years. Now Jesús is the sixth generation to be involved at C.V.N.E, a bodega that strives to make wines with long aging potential.

CUNE (coo-nay) is the colloquial pronunciation of the acronym for Compañía Vinicola del Norte de España (the Northern Spanish Wine Company), or C.V.N.E. It was used so prevalently that the company, founded near the railroad station in Haro in 1879, started using CUNE as a brand name.

Jesús has the same sweet demeanor and lack of pretention as his father, so it is not surprising that of his five siblings he is the one continuing the winemaking tradition. Jesús remembers his father playing hide-and-seek with him in the vineyards as a child and recalls being fascinated by the laboratory at the bodega with its flasks and beakers filled with colorful liquids. Curiously enough, laboratory analysis was where Jesús first entered the wine business a few decades later.

Jesús's childhood memories are augmented by other lessons gleaned from his father as an adolescent. His father told him to look to the vines for answers in life, and that is what he has done. Jesús is totally involved with the land. He will digress from a conversation to explain the prehistoric geological formation of the Ebro River valley millions of years ago and its impact on the soil. This total absorption in the land is intrinsic to his nature, as it is to many vintners in Rioja.

Jesús studied viticulture and enology and after finishing his studies began to work at C.V.N.E. under the tutelage of Basilio Izquierdo, whom he greatly respects. He then moved to the Contino estate started in the 1970s by his mentor and became its technical director in 1998. A few of the wines of which he is proudest are his first Gran Reserva, which he released in 1996, and his 100 percent Graciano produced from vines planted by his father.

BARREL AGING AND
TYPES OF OAK

Barrel aging in oak is specified as part of the definition of a Crianza, Reserva, or Gran Reserva wine. The first use of cask aging dates back to the late eighteenth century; it was in 1786 that Don Manuel Quintano (see page 147), a priest and winemaker born in Labastida, brought oak casks back to Rioja from his enological studies in Bordeaux.

All the barrels used in Rioja are 60 gallons (225 liters) by law, and some bodegas still employ coopers on site. Currently there are more than 1.2 million barrels filled with wine in the cellars of the DOCa Rioja bodegas.

Wine enthusiasts and professional enologists alike frequently argue the relative merits of using American oak versus French oak for barrel aging. The vintners in Rioja use both, although the vast majority—almost 90 percent— use American oak. In addition, some bodegas use oak from countries such as Hungary.

New wood releases tannin into the wine from its pores and slows the breakdown of the red pigments in the wine to preserve its luscious red color. Over time, however, tiny amounts of oxygen enter the cask through the pores of the wood and interact with the wine, which causes it to age. The aging process involves a softening of the fruit flavors in the wine and changes to the tannins. It also better integrates all the different flavor and texture elements of the wine.

There is no question that the type of wood used for aging helps define the character of the wine. American white oak is less porous than the French oak used in Rioja. Thus, less oxygen enters the barrel, and the wine develops more slowly. American oak is also much more flavorful than French oak, lending a noticeable vanilla aroma to the wine.

HOW TO READ A RIOJA WINE LABEL

Unlike in other DO regions of Spain, all the wines produced under the auspices of the DOCa Rioja are *vinos de calidad*, quality wines. There are no lesser categories such as *vinos de mesa* (table wines) or *vinos de la tierra* (regional wines). However, Spain has no such thing as national labeling; each DO region defines its wines individually. It is risky, therefore, to assume that *all* Crianza or Reserva wines are subjected to the same level of aging before release as in Rioja.

Within the DOCa Rioja, labeling rules do exist; the Rioja Regulatory Control Board enforces them. The meaning of the color-coded age labels is discussed on pages 130 to 132. Here is how to interpret the front label of a bottle of Rioja:

- **THE PROPRIETARY NAME** of the wine. This is the largest type on the label.

- **THE NAME OF THE BODEGA,** which can be smaller than the wine name. If there is no proprietary wine name, the bodega name can be the largest type, and it frequently includes a logo or crest.

- **THE NAME OF THE VILLAGE** where the wine was bottled.

- **THE NAME RIOJA,** which cannot be more than $^{4}/_{10}$ inch (10 mm) high and cannot be wider than half the width of the label. Directly beneath the word *Rioja* must be *Denominación de Origen Calificada*.

- **THE CLASSIFICATION OF THE WINE** (Crianza, Reserva, Gran Reserva) is optional, but most bodegas include this information.

- **THE VINTAGE YEAR.**

- **THE OTHER MANDATORY LABEL LISTINGS** are for the size of the bottle, the alcoholic content, the words "contains sulfites," an indication of the source such as "Product of Spain," and a seal of certification.

- **OCCASIONALLY A LIST OF THE GRAPES** in the blend. This is optional on the front label.

PREVIOUS PAGES: Bodegas Viña Real Barrel Aging Room

VINTAGES OF RIOJA WINE

The Rioja Regulatory Control Board utilizes a highly skilled tasting committee of more than fifty professionals engaged in a five-step process to assess the quality of a vintage. This information is posted on the organization's website, and here is the assessment for more than forty years of red wines.

E = excellent, VG = very good, G = good, S = satisfactory, A = average

1960: G	1973: G	1986: G	1999: G
1961: G	1974: G	1987: VG	2000: G
1962: VG	1975: VG	1988: G	2001: E
1963: S	1976: G	1989: G	2002: G
1964: E	1977: S	1990: G	2003: G
1965: A	1978: VG	1991: VG	2004: E
1966: S	1979: S	1992: G	2005: E
1967: S	1980: G	1993: G	2006: VG
1968: VG	1981: VG	1994: E	2007: VG
1969: S	1982: E	1995: E	2008: VG
1970: VG	1983: G	1996: VG	2009: VG
1971: A	1984: S	1997: G	2010: E
1972: A	1985: G	1998: VG	

STYLES OF RIOJA WINE

Although law dictates the aging levels of wines in Rioja, there is great diversity within each category as to the style of the wine. This diversity extends to a wide range of palates, not to mention price points.

Answers about style can be gleaned from a number of sources. A trusted wine merchant or sommelier in a restaurant can be tapped for reliable knowledge, and reviews in wine magazines and on websites can also be good sources of information about style. But the best sources are the vintners themselves. They are generally forthcoming and welcome interest in their wines, so feel free to go to their websites and contact them directly. Most of the styles outlined below are terms the winemakers of Rioja and knowledgeable merchants and sommeliers know and use. Modern Classic is a category that fills a gap between Classic wines and the more recent styles.

Each producer has its own style and production secrets, so if you are aging your wines, it is best to drink them at the recommended age for peak development but also to be familiar with the producer since any particular wine may reach "optimal drinking time" before or after the guidelines. Still, even a few years after the recommended aging time many Riojas still drink very well, with fruit and acidity both present and in balance.

One aspect of Rioja wine style remains constant: The wines are made from indigenous grapes. By law, the vineyards in Rioja are planted only with these grapes,

which are discussed at length in Chapter 4. That sets wines from Rioja apart from the homogenizing globalization that has taken place in many regions around the world.

Wines in Rioja have one foot resting on the region's heritage and the other on exploring the future. To quote Fernando Remírez de Ganuza of Bodegas Remírez de Ganuza, whose 2004 Gran Reserva was awarded 100 points by Robert Parker, Rioja's greatest goal and challenge for the twenty-first century should be "to strive for perfection in all we do, from the vineyard through to the bottle."

CLASSICS

These wines are as timeless as a strand of pearls, a black dress, or the pleated front of a tuxedo shirt. Many of the classics are made by the centenary bodegas. The grapes for these wines often are sourced from different parcels and subzones in Rioja. The wines are typically at least 75 percent Tempranillo, with the remaining percentage consisting of Mazuelo, Garnacha, and Graciano.

MODERN CLASSICS

These wines are today's continuation of the traditions of Rioja winemaking, and they are plentiful in the contemporary marketplace. They contain grapes collected from parcels of land in all three subregions. There is much innovation in each of the subregions today, and this is reflected in Modern Classics, which often are made with 90 to 100 percent Tempranillo and are aged in French oak.

ELENA ADELL

When Elena Adell, a soft-spoken woman who wields tremendous power in Rioja, became a viticulturist in the early 1980s, it was difficult for a woman to get an interview for a job, let alone a job. This native of Agoncillo is now chief winemaker at Bodegas Campo Viejo, formerly known as Bodegas Juan Alcorta. Her position encompasses the production at Bodegas Ysios in Rioja Alavesa and all the other properties of Campo Viejo.

She projects a sense of ease and confidence as she speaks, belying the fact that her decisions have a tremendous impact on the way the wines of Rioja are perceived around the world. Aromatics, expression, balance, and a flavorful palate experience are fundamental to her design of wines.

Elena recalls that her childhood introduction to wine consisted of dipping cookies into a glass of it while sitting with her grandfather. This memory for her is a reflection of Riojan culture. Not only was the wine delicious, it also provided her with pleasure. Providing pleasure is her goal for her wines, too.

Agoncillo, where she grew up, remains the center of an annual cornucopia of produce. She knew from a very early age that she wanted to work the land, which she has done since her graduation from university. She candidly admits to feeling the pressure of her position—she hardly has time to get a stuffy nose, let alone to make a mistake. It has not lessened her delight.

She thinks being a winemaker is so stimulating because it allows women to combine technical knowledge with creativity in decision making. For her, therein lies both a feminine challenge and beauty.

SUBZONAL

This category of wines represents a departure from the traditional Riojan approach of blending grapes from the three subregions; they contain grapes from only one subregion. There is a great range of mesoclimates in Rioja, and this approach capitalizes on location and the topographic diversity of a single zone.

SINGLE ESTATE

Unlike in regions such as Bordeaux, where the land holdings of a single château can be vast, the laws of inheritance as well as tradition in Rioja have maintained the convention of many small parcels of land. In this way, the growers of Rioja remain closely in touch with their land and their grapes. The concept of wines coming only from vineyards within the estate property is both new to Rioja and relatively rare. Single-estate wines are also subzonal. The word *finca*, which means "estate" in Spanish, is often part of the winery name on these bottles or is included on the label as a descriptive term. Barón de Ley, Campillo, Contino, and Finca Valpiedra are some bodegas that are bottling single-estate wines.

SINGLE VINEYARD

The production of wine from a specific vineyard or plot is another new trend in Rioja and one that is rising at an accelerated pace. The vast number of vineyard climates and terroirs in Rioja provides great diversity between one wine and the next in this category.

Single-vineyard wines are made in most wine regions of the world as a way to showcase exceptional fruit that reflects a specific terroir.

HIGH-EXPRESSION WINES, VINOS DE AUTOR

These wines, bottled very young, began being produced in Rioja around 1997. This new style of winemaking, often called New World, arose in response to worldwide trends. These are high-alcohol wines with a lot of extraction—thick and heavy in the mouth—and often show some aggressive use of French oak. They are a fashion of today, and although they carry a Cosecha label, they stand apart from standard Cosechas (see page 130).

THE ROLE OF THE RIOJA REGULATORY CONTROL BOARD

Founded in 1926, nine years before the similar French *appellation d'origine contrôlée* (AOC) system, the Rioja Regulatory Control Board oversees the production of wine; the labels it grants to bodegas are seals you can trust. The DO system in Spain recognizes the regional designation of the wine-producing area, but the control board goes far beyond that to administer stringent quality control. It controls vineyard yields, vineyard care, grape varieties, aging, and production. It maintains meticulous records, and its stance is as firm and clear as the mountains that frame this bountiful region.

THE ASSOCIATION OF FAMILY WINERIES

Family is a powerful concept in all societies, and it is of great importance in Rioja. It is more common than not to find a bodega run by the fourth or fifth generation of a family.

Now numbering more than forty family-run wineries, from very small to very large producers, the Association of Family Wineries (Bodegas Familiares de Rioja) was founded in 1991 to preserve the sense of family vineyards. Eighty percent of the members are descended from agriculturists in the region. The motto of the organization is "the hand by which the land becomes wine."

This embodies the spirit of the family winery that lives in the vineyards of Rioja and aspires to maintain the traditions of previous generations alongside the innovation of today, to hold on to the essence of Rioja and what it means to be Riojan. Organizations like this one are especially important in the face of the slow but ongoing globalization of wine.

Called the *Consejo Regulador* in Spanish, the control board is responsible for every bottle of wine and tracks wines by the bottle number. It grants an average of 350 million numbered labels annually, and to obtain a bottle number the winery must fulfill a rigorous program of checks by inspectors both in the vineyards and at the winery. Each and every bottle can be tracked by its number and corresponding record of inspections; that is why the guarantee-of-origin seal is one a consumer can trust.

This process of quality control accelerates during the harvest. More than two hundred inspectors are hired by the Board Inspection Services to follow the grapes. They monitor the transfer of grapes from grower to bodega, control the borders of the wine region, verify the quality of the grapes, and observe the weighing of all grapes on scales at the winemaking centers. These centers are now computerized, which makes communication with the control board's office in Logroño instantaneous; in earlier eras the inspectors would have to drive to the office with their logs.

To grow or sell grapes with the right to use the DOCa Rioja label, the more than 18,000 vineyard owners must have a supporting document, the "Grape Grower's Record Book," in which the registered surface area of the vineyard and the maximum authorized grape output in kilograms must appear. In accordance with the regulations, the yield is kept to 6,500 kilograms (14,330 pounds) per hectare (2.47 acres) for red varieties and 9,000 kilograms (19,841 pounds) per hectare for white varieties.

Consensus does govern process for large institutions, and today there is consensus among Riojan wine producers that the presence and work of the control board have strongly influenced Rioja's quality and definition. In a recent survey, a resounding 94 percent of Rioja's producers responded that the control board enforces their regulations with a signature of trust.

A HISTORY OF QUALITY CONTROL

Whether a chef, a vintner, or a cobbler, everyone in Rioja is concerned about quality control. The wine production regulations maintained by the control board today follow precepts dating back centuries to protect Rioja's wines and support the wine industry.

Archives in Logroño's city hall document laws in the eighteenth century that forbade the mixing of previous years' wines with the current vintage; it was punishable by incarceration. In 1729 the *Junta de Cosecheros* (Growers Association) was formed, which soon evolved into the Royal Economic Society of Castilian Growers. Associations like this one sought to protect the interests of their vines and simultaneously—and quite astutely—established roadways and bridges to transport the grapes from the three subregions to the bodegas and then transport their wines to market.

Cities within the region also acted. Laguardia, a charming medieval village and one of Rioja's two largest wine municipalities, prohibited the importation of wine from Navarre, and in the capital of Logroño taxation systems and other regulations were put into place to protect growers.

The number of societies increased in the second half of the eighteenth century. In 1765, the *Junta de Cosecheros Riojanos* (Growers Association of Rioja) was formed in Fuenmayor; this was followed in 1785 by the *Real Sociedad Bascongada de Amigos del País* (the Basque Royal Society of Friends). This second society administered an essay contest in 1785 on how to make better wine. At the time there were predominantly two schools of thought. On one side were the traditional *cosecheros* who wanted to keep vineyard expansion and winemaking methods as they were. A rustic style of Rioja was what they were accustomed to, and the new methods being proposed, including the use of oak barrels for aging, were expensive.

Battling for the other side was Manuel Quintano. A noted cleric and the scion of a noble family of Labastida that produced wine, Manuel traveled to Bordeaux for the harvest in 1785 and 1786. He returned from the Médoc with ideas on better ways to both make and transport wine—the Bordeaux method—which he documented in several papers. His essay won the grand prize of a silver medal in the Basque Royal Society of Friends contest.

The oak aging Quintano espoused made the wine more expensive, which fueled the flames of class division among winemakers. The wines made using the Bordeaux method sold for 24 reales, while the common wines cost 6. The issue went to court, and the Quintano family was accused of adopting the production method to increase the separation between the rich and the poor. After three years of arguments, the court ruled in 1804 that the Quintano family and its allies could not sell wines made and aged with the Bordeaux method.

It took almost sixty years for that decision to be reversed. It was in 1858 that Don Camilio Hurtado de Amézaga, the Marqués de Riscal, was asked by the Diputación Foral de Álava (the Provincial Council of Álava) to find an expert in Bordeaux to teach winemaking techniques to the region's vintners. That man was Jean Pineau of Château Lanessan, who spread the gospel of oak aging. By the end of the nineteenth century the wines from both Marqués de Riscal and Marqués de Murrieta were being aged in oak barrels.

Pedro de Atalay, a wine merchant in Havana, Cuba, submitted another winning essay; he discussed the importance of adequate barrels for aging and transatlantic transport. During the eighteenth century, Spain controlled many territories around the world, so the ability to ship wines was paramount to the success of the industry.

MARÍA JOSÉ LÓPEZ DE HEREDIA

The López de Heredia family has been winemakers in the Rioja Alta for more than a century, so it is only natural that María José, a member of the fourth generation, has childhood memories of vineyards. But it is her childhood Sundays that really stand out for her.

On that day of rest the family would pile into their little gray Morris Mini and head to the Viña Tondonia vineyard, a parcel of almost 250 acres (100 hectares) on the right bank of the Ebro River. Her great-grandfather had purchased the vineyard and replanted it in 1914, after the phylloxera epidemic. It was an arduous process that almost provoked him to sell the winery and flee Rioja, as many of his neighbors did at that time.

While her father, Pedro, worked in the vineyard, María José and her siblings—one of whom, Mercedes, is now the winemaker at R. López de Heredia (see page 165)—would play as their mother read magazines. Like all children, they would tire of their games, so they would sit in the car waiting for their father, after whose arrival they could drive to have lunch in nearby Tirgo. María José's success at the bodega, where she is now managing director, came from this ingrained sense of responsibility and desire. Her passion for and dedication

to the bodega run through her veins; this winery is her life. She would chat about family history and the winery in the middle of the night if you called her. She works tirelessly traveling the world as an ambassador for her wines, which have such a Riojan essence.

When María José speaks of her father it is with an almost superhuman reverence, and Pedro López de Heredia is quite a man to have had as a mentor. He was a strong and respected voice for the Rioja Regulatory Control Board, but even more important, he is a significant individual who has shaped the region and its wines today; all in the region utter the name of the bodega with hushed reverence.

María José has learned from her father's example and now continues the many projects begun by her grandfather. He knew that his visions would require generations of work to accomplish—she describes him as having a "well-furnished mind." But it is up to her generation to maintain the traditions of a bodega that is almost a shrine unto itself in Rioja.

ENOLOGICAL STATION OF HARO

The Enological Station was established in Haro in 1892. The site was selected because of its proximity to some of the emerging bodegas of the time, which are among the constellation of centenary bodegas today. It was envisioned as a multidisciplinary center capable of providing many services to growers and winemakers for experimentation, education, analysis, and elaboration (the making of wine).

The Enological Station has operated for 120 years without interruption and today is a resource for wine regions and producers around the world as well as serving as the official analysis laboratory for the Rioja Regulatory Control Board. It has rigorously pursued expanding its chemical analysis services and now receives more than fifteen thousand samples and conducts more than 120,000 analyses annually.

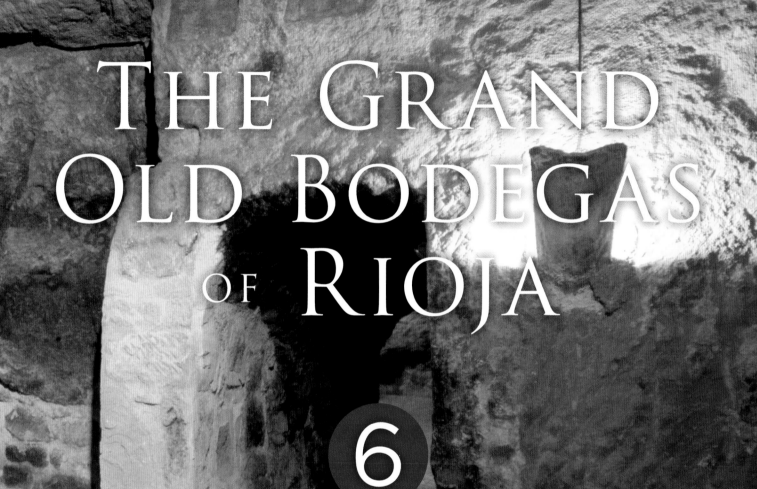

The Grand Old Bodegas of Rioja

6

The bodegas and wines of the DOCa Rioja deserve a book of their own, but this chapter includes only a sampling of Riojan wineries that are more than fifty years old; Chapter 7 covers newer bodegas. All the bodegas listed here have distribution in the United States.

Although new bodegas are established regularly in Rioja, the current elegant style of the wine, based on the unique relationship between the land and the Tempranillo grape, goes back to the mid-nineteenth century. Critical to the rise of bodegas at that time was the establishment of the railroad, which arrived in Logroño in 1863 and Haro in 1880 and linked both cities to the port city of Bilbao, making Rioja wines accessible to the world.

There have been changes in ownership, name, and structure for many of these bodegas. Some are now part of international beverage conglomerates, whereas others remain in the hands of the families that founded them. Some have ventured forth from Rioja to start wineries in other DO regions of Spain, and others have grown by acquiring more land and wineries within Rioja. But all these wineries, even if they have added modern, high-expression wines to their offerings, still produce wines that reflect a rich Riojan wine culture. To quote the wine writer Matt Kramer, "A wine culture is not an inevitable outgrowth of any other kind of culture, no matter how refined or evolved." Rioja's wine culture reflects its singular tradition of Reservas and Gran Reservas, its unique terroir, and the rich heart, soul, and soil of this region.

There is a group of a dozen wineries that are now more than a century old; some were making wine for a few decades before phylloxera devastated the region. They are marked with this symbol in the list below.

"Wines of note" refers to specific bottlings that have kept a special signature style throughout the years. Noticeably absent from this listing are vintages because of circulating inventories. However, references to great vintages, which are found on page 139, can provide additional insight. Many of the wines mentioned here fall in the Reserva category and deliver quality, value, and the ability to be enjoyed now or cellared for the short term or long term. The number of wine regions in the world that can claim these attributes for their wine is quite small.

BODEGAS BILBAÍNAS

YEAR FOUNDED: 1901

Wines of note: Viña Zaco, Viña Pomal Crianza, La Vicalanda Reserva

CHAPTER OPENER: Antique equipment, Bodegas Castillo de Sajazarra
PREVIOUS PAGES: La Rioja Alta
PREVIOUS RIGHT TOP: Ernest Hemingway at Bodegas Franco Españolas
PREVIOUS RIGHT BOTTOM: Marqués de Murrieta

The building in which this bodega is housed in Haro dates from 1859, when Sauvignon Frères et Cie built it and established a winery, having fled France and phylloxera. It was fortuitous that just as they wanted to return to France, a group of businessmen from Bilbao decided to buy a winery, and this tan structure became their base. Under the leadership of the wine merchant Santiago de Ugarte y Aurrecoechea, the bodega began in 1901. In 1997 the Codorníu Group purchased Bilbaínas and undertook a massive program of modernization.

Bodegas Bilbaínas (a centenary bodega) is the only bodega in Haro that is an estate property. In addition to the 90 hectares of vineyards inside the Haro Estate they own over 60 acres (150 hectares) of vineyards in Haro and Villalba de Rioja that meet approximately 70 percent of their needs; the remaining grapes are purchased from other growers. Current and talented winemaker Diego Pinilla juxtaposes nicely Bilbaínas history with his impressive international schooling and experience.

The bodega produces wines bottled with a variety of labels named after specific vineyards. Viña Pomal, which made its first appearance in 1908, is the name used for most of its Reserva and Gran Reserva wines as well as one Crianza. La Vicalanda, whose first vintage was 1994, is a high-expression wine with a brighter color and fruit than traditional Riojas. The bodega's third label, Viña Zaco, which carries a Cosecha back label, is a 100 percent Tempranillo. It is named for the oldest of the vineyards but was created just a few years ago.

NAVIGATING THE LISTINGS OF BODEGAS

Even within a straightforward alphabetical list there are exceptions to the rule, and this list contains a few. Bodegas sometimes are identified by the way they are commonly known instead of by their legal names. For example, the acronym C.V.N.E is used rather than what it represents (Compania Vinícola del Norte de España). The same is true for bodegas such as Marqués de Riscal, which is officially titled Bodegas de los Herederos del Marqués de Riscal.

Another idiosyncrasy is that the names of wineries that begin with the word *bodega* are listed by what follows that word, which is a description rather than a name. The same is true for wineries beginning with the word *finca*, which is appearing more often as wineries are making single-estate wines. However, wineries whose names begin with the article *El* or *La* have the article included.

Finally, wineries with personal names are are alphabetized by the given name rather than the surname. The same method is used in Chapter 7.

BODEGAS CAMPO VIEJO

YEAR FOUNDED: 1959

Wines of note: Campo Viejo Reserva, Dominio

In 2001 the bodega moved into a stunning modern building on a high plateau near Logroño with commanding views from all angles. Ignacio Quemada Sáenz-Badillos, an architect born in Logroño, designed the complex. The winery is divided into two parts; the visitors' center is all aboveground, whereas most of the winery is built into the rock, with only small sections appearing aboveground. The form of the buildings is simple; they achieve elegance with the geometric patterns on their surfaces.

The majority of the wines bear the label Campo Viejo. The Crianza, Reserva, and Gran Reserva are made from Tempranillo, Graciano, and Mazuelo; the white wine is 100 percent Viura; and the rosé is 100 percent Tempranillo. In addition to the Campo Viejo label, there are Reserva and Gran Reserva wines released as Marqués de Villamagna. Other labels are Alcorta for Crianza wines and Dominio, a high-expression wine.

The bodega changed its name from Bodegas Juan Alcorta in 2009 to celebrate the fiftieth anniversary of its signature brand. Grapes have been grown on this site in Villar de Arnedo in Rioja Baja since Roman times, when vineyard land was given as a reward to returning soldiers. The name means "old fields," and this was where José Ortigüela started the vineyard in 1959 with Bernardo Beristain and Juan Alcorta. The first wine, which was made in Ortigüela's stone winery, was released in 1961.

C.V.N.E (COMPANIA VINÍCOLA DEL NORTE DE ESPAÑA)

YEAR FOUNDED: 1879

Wines of note: Imperial Gran Reserva, Viña Real Crianza, Contino Reserva, Contino 100% Graciano

C.V.N.E began in 1879, and by 1900 there were more than eighty thousand bottles aging in its cellars in Haro, where this Rioja Alta winery still sits. The founders were the brothers Eusebio and Raimundo Real de Asúa, and the winery is now in the hands of the fifth generation of the family. Along the way the acronym was transformed to CUNE (**coo**-nay), which is now the way most of its wines are labeled.

For many decades the legendary winemaker Basilio Izquierdo and the viticulturist José Madrazo worked side by side making these wines, which many in the world appreciate as great classic Riojas. Current winemaker María Larrea took the torch from Basilio, who also established the Contino estate in 1973.

Contino is located in Rioja Alavesa and is owned by C.V.N.E.; this single-estate property has 153 acres (62 hectares) and boasts a romantic fifteenth-century manor house that has been restored and now serves as an aging cellar and guesthouse. All the Contino wines are made entirely from grapes grown on the estate. In addition to a Reserva and a Gran Reserva and a white wine bottled with the name Contino, there is also Contino Graciano, one of the first 100 percent Graciano wines from Rioja. The modern wine from this vineyard is labeled Viña del Olivo.

Back in Haro, there is a CUNE white, Monopole, and a CUNE Crianza, but CUNE's flagship wines were always the Imperial and Viña Real, which traditionally were differentiated not only by the vineyards and bottle shapes but by the blends. When a greater percentage of Garnacha occupied Rioja's vineyards, the Viña Real label often included up to 30 percent Garnacha.

The Viña Real (Royal Vineyard) wine received "royal" treatment when the group decided to build a separate bodega for this label in 1989. It was designed by the French architect Phillipe Mazières, who had done work in Bordeaux for both Château Margaux and Château d'Yquem. This circular structure draws one in; it is magnetic and majestic, in the shape of a giant wooden barrel. The wines are aged in the center, and the huge fermentation tanks are placed around the periphery. The Viña Real label is affixed to a Burgundy-shaped bottle for the Crianza, Reserva, Gran Reserva, and white wines. The other wine is called Pagos de Viña Real, and it is a high-expression wine.

DINASTÍA VIVANCO

YEAR FOUNDED: 1915
Wines of note: Vivanco Blanco,
Vivanco Mazuelo, Vivanco Reserva

The foundation date of 1915 for this winery is technically accurate but somewhat misleading. While Pedro Vivanco González began making wine in that year, it was really for his family and for a few neighbors if there was extra. It was his grandson, Pedro Vivanco Paracuellos, who took what had been a slowly growing business and made it wildly successful in the 1970s, when he acquired vineyards and winery interests in the region.

He acquired the site of the present bodega in Briones in

1985 and began construction of Bodegas Dinastía Vivanco in 1990. The current winemaker is Pedro's very qualified son, Rafael Vivanco. Rafael studied winemaking in France and has brought together a dynamic team. His winemaking exhibits both heritage and innovation, and it will be very interesting to watch his signature unfold in Riojan history.

J. Marino Pascual, a Riojan architect, designed the current bodega and museum (see page 162). The bodega is below ground except for an octagonal cupola at ground level that is enveloped in vineyards and offers wonderful views of the valley.

All of Dinastía Vivanco's wines are sold in bottles whose design is based on an eighteenth-century shape, the prototype for which is on display in the museum. Under the Vivanco label are a rosé made from 85 percent Tempranillo and 15 percent Garnacha as well as a white wine. The Dinastía Vivanco brand includes a 100 percent Tempranillo Crianza and a Reserva of 90 percent Tempranillo and 10 percent Graciano, all picked from vines at least thirty-five years old. The Vivanco Colección label is

placed on bottles of 100 percent Graciano, 100 percent Mazuelo, and 100 percent Garnacha wines.

BODEGAS FAUSTINO

YEAR FOUNDED: 1861

Wines of note: Faustino VII Cosecha, Faustino V Reserva

A winery this old could be called an Old Master, and Bodegas Faustino features likenesses of paintings by Rembrandt on many of its labels. The bodega's founder, Eleuterio Martínez Arzok, bought a house and vineyard in Oyón in Rioja Alavesa, and this remains one of the largest family-owned wineries in Rioja. His son, Faustino Martínez Pérez de Albéniz, was born in 1904, the year Rioja was stricken with phylloxera. He began to bottle wines in the early 1930s, when wine was more commonly sold in bulk and bottling was the exception rather than the norm.

Faustino's son, Julio Faustino Martínez, took over in 1957, and the first Faustino wines, named in honor of his father, were released in 1960. Faustino acquired two other bodegas, Campillo in 1990 and Marqués de Vitoria in 1995. The Faustino wines are more classic in style, as are those from Campillo, whereas the Marqués de Vitoria wines are more modern. In this latter camp are Ecco, a 100 percent Tempranillo wine made with grapes picked from vines at least thirty years old and aged in American oak, and Original, also made from 100 percent Tempranillo.

A GLEAMING CITY OF WINE

On a sunny day as you round a bend in the road and pass through the medieval village of Elciego, your eye focuses on a bright pink object gleaming in the distance. That is your first view of the breathtaking Marqués de Riscal Hotel, the centerpiece of the bodega's City of Wine.

Harvest is naturally in "high season," but when you pull up to the hotel in any season and take a deep breath, the olfactory welcome you receive is the scent of the grape must that impregnates the air. It reminds you why you came here in the first place. As time passes, you realize this place is an all-encompassing sensory experience. Smell, sight, taste, and textures coexist in almost organic luxury enveloped in a homage to and celebration of wine. The hotel, which opened in 2006, sits atop the cellars of the bodega, and the eighteenth-century bodega itself is adjacent to the hotel.

The building was designed by the famed Canadian-born architect Frank O. Gehry, and like his spectacular Guggenheim Museum in nearby Bilbao, the hotel is covered with bands made from tons of titanium that look like flows of ribbon candy. At first glance it is a surreal visual experience.

It is not just that it is a five-star hotel in a vineyard that makes the Riscal so magnificent. It is the aura of peace that represents the relaxed Riojan state of mind. Everything is impeccable, and the views appear as if they were exquisite landscape oil paintings on your living room wall.

A SPECTACULAR CELEBRATION
OF ALL THINGS WINE

Far from even the small city of Logroño, let alone a major world capital, is the greatest wine museum in the world. The Dinastía Vivanco Museum of the Culture of Wine is situated amid fields of lavender and surrounded by vineyards at the bottom of a hill. Far above it sits the medieval walled village of Briones in Rioja Alta.

The palatial building is also an epicenter for wine education, history, culture, and celebration. The museum welcomes 150,000 visitors annually from around the world, and it should hold a prominent position on every wine aficionado's lifetime to-do list.

In a region where harvest was historically approached as a family affair, the museum, which opened in 2004, mirrors this idea and encourages visitors of all ages to explore the world of wine through the many exhibits, which include interactive and sensory experiences. The museum is like nothing else you will find in Spain—or in any other country; it is worth a detour to Rioja for the novice or the expert to spend a day there.

The idea for the museum came to Pedro Vivanco Paracuellos as a way of living his motto: "to give back to wine what wine has given to us." Generosity of soul is the ruling principle of his life. He brings melons from his garden to share with colleagues and friends; he amassed perhaps the greatest wine-related art collection in the world and shares that too.

The impressive museum has three levels connected by comfortable walking ramps that make the building handicapped accessible; the museum has also been praised for its tags in Braille. The Vivanco family have been ardent collectors—of everything from bottles to grape presses—for more than forty years. Pedro's son, Santiago, has formed many of the collections.

On the practical side is a collection of winemaking artifacts, including a grape press that is estimated to be almost two thousand years old. Myriad vineyard tools, baskets to carry grapes, and bottles to hold wine dating back to the Romans are included in these galleries. Then there are galleries that are more like a traditional museum for artworks dating back to the third millennium BCE and including pieces as modern as Picasso ceramics. The quality of these artworks would make them welcome in any of the world's most noted museums.

In addition to the artworks there are films showing aspects of winemaking, from a year in the life of a vineyard and how to make a barrel to a spectacular short filmed inside a fermentation tank in which you can hear as well as see the wine fermenting. The interactive area that seems to attract visitors of all ages is the olfactory cove. Here visitors can dab small pieces of paper into oils formulated to represent the various aroma notes in wine—from pineapple to star anise and from lavender to oak.

The museum finale is, appropriately, a collection of five thousand corkscrews dating back to the late eighteenth century, along with decanters and wine goblets. The experience of visiting the museum is well worth a toast!

BODEGAS FEDERICO PATERNINA

YEAR FOUNDED: 1896

Wines of note: Banda Dorada Blanco, Banda Azul Crianza

Federico de Paternina Josué merged three small wineries in his quaint village of Ollauri in Rioja Alta in 1896. The cellars were tunneled into rock and are still referred to as the Cathedral of Wine. They descend more than 40 feet (12 meters); some of the preexisting tunnels date to the sixteenth century and meander for almost 2,000 feet (600 meters), a maze of mesmerizing and majestic aging cellars where one is serenaded by Gregorian chants. Paternina, who was one of the younger sons of the Marqués de Terán, sold the bodega to a banker from Logroño in 1919. The banker continued to amass properties, including the Catholic Farmers' Union Cooperative in 1922, and moved the operations for the bodega to Haro. Paternina remained as a consultant to the bodega until

his death in the 1930s, with a consultant from Bordeaux, Étienne Labatut, working alongside him. The Paternina bodega in Ollauri was a favorite haunt of Ernest Hemingway during his time in Spain after his close friend Antonio Ordoñez, the legendary bullfighter, introduced him to his favorite bodegas.

The major labels of Bodegas Federico Paternina today are Clisos, which is 100 percent Tempranillo; Banda Verde, a Cosecha; Banda Azul and Banda Oro, two Crianza wines; Banda Roja, a Reserva; Clos, a Reserva; and Conde de los Andes, a Gran Reserva. Additionally, they produce Banda Dorada, a white wine made with Viura, and a delicate semidulce white, Graciela.

LA RIOJA ALTA

YEAR FOUNDED: 1890

Wines of note: Viña Alberdi, Viña Ardanza, 904 Gran Reserva

In the boom years when phylloxera had devastated France but had yet to arrive in Spain, many French investors built wineries around the newly opened railroad station in Haro, and Albert Viguier was one of them. In 1890 he sold to a consortium of five Basque and Riojan growers, who became the Sociedad Vinicola de la Rioja Alta. They began making wines in the Bordeaux style and changed the name to La Rioja Alta a year later.

In the late nineteenth century, in-house coopers manufactured all the casks at the winery, and the winery returned to this tradition in 2002. Although the company is now publicly traded, the fifth generation of the original families is still involved with the business. La Rioja Alta is a true great classic bodega. These wines age tremendously in the bottle. The 1,200-acre (475-hectare) estate with Tempranillo vines is in Rioja Alta, and the Garnacha for blending is grown on a 155-acre (53-hectare) parcel in Rioja Baja. In general, it is a signature style of La Rioja Alta to hold aged wines much longer than the DOCa requires.

The company's trademarked label of the Oja River depicted with four oak trees was registered in 1902 and has not changed. The Viña Ardanza label, for which the bodega is best known, began in 1942. In the early 1970s Viña Arana and Viña Alberdi were introduced as labels, and Marqués de Haro joined them in 1985. The winery also owns the Torre de Oña estate in the Alavesa. The Viña Ardanza Reserva and the 890 and 904 Gran Reservas are great classic Riojas.

LÓPEZ DE HEREDIA (R. LÓPEZ DE HEREDIA)

YEAR FOUNDED: 1877

Wines of note: Viña Tondonia Reserva Blanco, Viña Tondonia Rosado, Viña Tondonia Gran Reserva

R. López de Heredia is one of the few bodegas in Rioja that remain authentic family wineries, in this case with the fourth generation of descendants of Don Rafael López de Heredia y Landeta in charge today. Rafael was born in Chile in 1857 to parents whose roots were in the Alavesa, and the family moved to Spain in 1869. He discovered his love of wine while studying in France.

Today this fascinating bodega in Haro, the center of the Rioja Alta, boasts some of the region's most spectacular architecture, such as its tasting room, designed by Zaha Hadid, an avant-garde Iraqi architect. The adjoining nineteenth-century buildings house the oak casks, which are not just American and French; some of the oak comes from Bosnia and Cantabria.

High standards and reverence define this bodega, the family, and its prized vineyards. The various vineyards give their names to the wines. The Viña Tondonia line, named for a parcel of 250 acres (101 hectares) on the right bank of the Ebro, includes some of the only white Reserva and Gran Reserva wines made in Rioja, in addition to a red Reserva and a Gran Reserva and a singular rosé. The winery's other brands are also named for parcels of land in Rioja Alta; they are Viña Bosconia, Viña Cubillo, and Viña Gravonia. López de Heredia is another winery that holds its wines much longer than is required by law; these very old wines are readily available on the international market.

LUIS CAÑAS

YEAR FOUNDED: 1928

Wines of note: Luis Cañas Reserva, Hiru 3 Racimos

Although the winery is less than a century old, the Cañas family has been growing grapes on lands in Rioja Alavesa for more than two hundred years, and it shows in the bottle. They began bottling a full range of Crianza to Reserva wines in 1970. The family owns more than 200 acres (90 hectares) of its own vineyards and purchases grapes from a vintage list of suppliers who own more than 800 plots that total 500 acres (210 hectares).

Luis retired in 1989, and his son, Juan Luis Cañas, took over at the young age of thirty-three. This winery is a perfect example of the spirit of twenty-first-century Rioja in that the youngest generation has returned to the winery from another profession instead of selling. By 1994 a new winery had been built, followed four years later by a major

LEFT: Tasting room at Bodegas R. López de Heredia

aging cellar. In the tradition of the Alavesa, some wines are made using carbonic maceration (see page 93), but today their greatest wines are barrel-aged subzonal bottlings.

The Luis Cañas label appears on a wide range of bottles, including a Gran Reserva made with 95 percent Tempranillo and a barrel-fermented white wine that is 90 percent Viura and 10 percent Malvasía. The Amaren label appears on a Reserva made from 100 percent Tempranillo as well as a wine made from 100 percent Graciano. The wine the family considers its flagship, however, is labeled Hiru 3 Racimos; *hiru* is the Basque word for "three," and *racimos* means "bunches of grapes." The wine is made from Tempranillo picked from sixty-year-old vines.

 ## MARQUÉS DE MURRIETA

YEAR FOUNDED: 1852

Wines of note: Capellania, Marqués de Murrieta Reserva, Castillo de Ygay Gran Reserva

The original founder of this bodega, Luciano Francisco Ramón de Murrieta, was born in Peru in 1822 and moved with his family as a young child to London, where he spent time with his uncle, General Rivero de Murrieta. In 1844 he moved to Spain, where he decided to become a winemaker, having seen the huge market potential of export sales. After studying in Bordeaux he started making wine in Rioja, and 100 barrels of his first vintage of 1852 was exported to Mexico and Cuba.

By 1878 he had purchased the now-legendary Ygay estate close to Logroño. Upon his death as a bachelor in 1911, the bodega was inherited by his nephew, Julián de Olivares, who sold the estate in 1977 to Vicente Cebrián-Sagarriga, Count of Creixell. His son, V. Dalmau Cebrián-Sagarriga, is now responsible for the bodega, and he has created a team of young, talented professionals to carry on the legendary tradition and heritage of Marqués de Murrieta. He personally embraces this role with great care and pride. In the summer of 2011 he completed a magnificent five-year renovation of the bodega.

More than 70 percent of the bodega's 741 acres (300 hectares) are planted with Tempranillo, with Graciano, Mazuelo, and Garnacha filling the remaining acreage. A sprinkling of Cabernet Sauvignon is allowed by the control board; it has been grown at Marqués de Murrieta for so long that its use is grandfathered there. The wines are aged primarily in American oak, usually in used casks that release less oak flavor and tannin into the wine.

The flagship wine of Marqués de Murrieta is the Castillo Ygay Tinto Gran Reserva Especial. Other labels are Dalmau Tinto Reserva, a high-expression wine launched in 1995; Marqués de Murrieta Tinto Reserva; and Capellania Blanco Reserva, made with Viura grapes grown in the Capellania vineyard.

MARQUÉS DE RISCAL (BODEGAS DE LOS HEREDEROS DEL MARQUÉS DE RISCAL)

YEAR FOUNDED: 1860

Wines of note: Próximo, Marqués de Riscal Reserva, Barón de Chirel

The history of Rioja has been intertwined with that of Bordeaux, especially during the late nineteenth century. There was French investment in Rioja when oïdium mold and then phylloxera afflicted the vineyards of France. Many of Rioja's legendary winemakers studied in Bordeaux and adopted such Bordelaise techniques as destemming grapes before fermentation and aging wine in oak. One of them was Don Camilio Hurtado de Amézaga, the

Marqués de Riscal, who moved to Bordeaux in 1836 during a period of civil unrest in Spain.

It was Don Camilio who hired the winemaker Jean Pineau to work with the winemakers of Álava, and after he returned to Spain in 1850, he sent the architect Ricardo Bellsola to Bordeaux to study the look of the châteaus there. Bellsola returned with the concept of aging cellars cut from stone with huge galleries for aging the wine, and Pineau's son was hired to construct the first oak barrels in Rioja.

Don Camilio's bodega released its first wines in 1860, two years after the founding of the winery. In 1868 Pineau's contract with Álava expired, and he joined the staff of the winery. The connection with Bordeaux remains strong; among the consultants to Marqués de Riscal are Guy Guimberteau of the Bordeaux Wine Institute and Paul Pontallier of Château Margaux.

All wines produced in Rioja are red. Most bottles from the winery carry the name Marqués de Riscal, and many are still wrapped in *malla*, the wire netting introduced in the late nineteenth century by Don Camilio to protect the integrity of the wine for export. In addition to the historic Reserva and Gran Reserva wines, there is a nice rosé and a relatively young wine named Próximo. Other, more modern wines are released under the labels Barón de Chirel, one of Don Camilio's other titles, and Frank Gehry Selección, a high-expression 100 percent Tempranillo named for the famed architect who designed the hotel on the winery's property.

 # MARTÍNEZ LACUESTA

YEAR FOUNDED: 1895

Wines of note: Martínez Lacuesta Blanco, Martínez Lacuesta Reserva

Félix Martínez Lacuesta was a well-known lawyer and politician in Haro who sat on many committees dealing with vines and wines. In 1895 he and his brothers started a bodega in an area that was then like a suburb of Haro, although it is now part of the center of the city. Much of their early production was exported to former Spanish colonies such as Cuba and Mexico; later the wines were sold mainly on the domestic market, and this remains the case. Today the third generation is in charge of running this family business. The largest change has been the recent construction of a commanding state-of-the-art facility on the outskirts of Haro.

The flagship of the bodega's wines is Ventilla 71, named for the address of the original building in Haro. The other wines are bottled with Martínez Lacuesta labels and include Crianzas, classic Reservas, and Gran Reservas as well as a white Rioja. All are examples of great Classic Riojas.

BODEGAS MONTECILLO

YEAR FOUNDED: 1874

Wines of note: Montecillo Crianza, Montecillo Gran Reserva

Rioja was experiencing economic prosperity in the mid-1870s when Celestino Navajas Matute first purchased the land for his bodega. His two sons, Gregorio and Alejandro, who had learned winemaking in Bordeaux, used the name Hijos de Celestino Najavas for their markedly French-style wines. It was Celestino's grandson, José-Luís, who changed the name of the bodega in 1947. El Montecillo is a hill on the outskirts of Fuenmayor in Rioja Alta, where the winery is located. In 1973 the bodega was purchased by Osborne y Cía, the regal sherry firm, and this commenced a new era for the philosophy and wines of Montecillo.

A pioneer in monovarietal Tempranillos of Rioja, Bodegas Montecillo owns no vineyards; it purchases grapes for its 100 percent Tempranillo wines from a network of suppliers, and in years in which the quality is not up to the winemaker's standards, no wine is made. Today Montecillo makes a red Crianza, a Reserva, and a Gran Reserva, all of which are bottled under its name. These wines are great examples of Modern Classics.

BODEGAS MUGA

YEAR FOUNDED: 1932

Wines of note: Muga Reserva, Torre Muga, Muga Rosado

The history of Bodegas Muga begins between the end of phylloxera in Rioja and the start of decades of civil unrest in Spain and all of Europe. But this story has a very happy ending, with the third generation of the Muga family currently in charge. Jorge Muga is the winemaker at this winery in the center of Haro in Rioja Alta.

The bodega is made from stone and oak, and it is the oak that is symbolic of the bodega in many ways. There is an artisanal cooper's workshop inside the bodega, which has more than fourteen thousand barrels for aging, made from three different types of French oak, plus American, Hungarian, and even Russian oak. There are no stainless steel, fiberglass, or concrete tanks anywhere in the building.

The bodega's 620 acres (250 hectares) of vineyards are situated in the folds of the Obarenes Mountains on a series of terraced plots. In addition, they purchase grapes from 370 acres (150 hectares) of vineyards whose viticulture they are able to oversee closely.

Most of the wines are bottled under the Muga name. They include a Reserva that is 70 percent Tempranillo and 20 percent Garnacha, with the remainder made up of Mazuelo and Graciano. There is also a white wine that is 90 percent Viura and 10 percent Malvasía aged in French oak and a rosé made from 60 percent Garnacha, 30 percent Viura, and 10 percent Tempranillo. The Prado Enea Gran Reserva is 80 percent Tempranillo with Garnacha, Mazuelo, and Graciano accounting for the balance.

BODEGAS PALACIO

YEAR FOUNDED: 1894

Wines of note: Cosme Palacio Tinto, Glorioso Reserva

In retrospect, starting a bodega in the 1890s, just as phylloxera was arriving in Rioja, could be deemed an unfortunate choice. But that is when Cosme Palacio y Bermejillo, a successful Bilbao businessman, and his brother, Manuel, began what is now Bodegas Palacio. Their father, Ángel, purchased the first vineyards near Laguardia in Rioja Alavesa in 1863. Bodegas Palacio's first release was in 1894.

When phylloxera hit, Cosme moved his operation to Castile-Leon, where phylloxera was not as prevalent, and made Rioja-style wines there until he could return to Rioja. The bodega's original building is now a lovely hotel, and in addition to the bodega's own 420 acres (170 hectares) of vineyard, it buys grapes from all three subregions in Rioja.

The bodega left the family's hands in 1972 and was purchased by the Canadian-based Seagram. In 1987 the management engaged the famed French wine consultant Michel Rolland, who redirected Bodegas Palacio to the standard of quality it achieves today.

Bodega Palacio's Glorioso wines date back to 1928. These classic Riojas include a Crianza, a Reserva, and a Gran Reserva aged in French oak. But Bodegas Palacio is continually innovating as well. Milflores, a high-expression Cosecha, is the latest addition to its brands. Other labels are Cosme Palacio, a handcrafted flagship wine aged in new French oak, and Bodegas Palacio Reserva Especial, for which the grapes are hand-selected only from old vines.

BODEGAS PALACIOS REMONDO

YEAR FOUNDED: 1948

Wines of note: Plácet, La Montesa

This family with roots in Alfaro in Rioja Baja has been making wine for more than three hundred years and is using its position as one of the leading growers in that subregion to elevate the region's bodegas in the twenty-first century.

The origin of the present winery dates to 1945, when José Palacios Remondo set up a business that emerged in 1948 as Bodegas Palacios Remondo. He and his wife had three daughters and six sons, four of whom went into the wine business. Antonio, the eldest, stayed in Rioja as the heir apparent, and his two brothers and a sister went to other DO regions of Spain after completing their winemaking studies. In 2000 Álvaro returned to Rioja and became the winemaker at Palacios Remondo. The 247-acre (100-hectare) vineyard is on a slope that faces south and east in the foothills of the Yerga Mountains at an altitude of 1,800 feet (550 meters).

La Vendimia is the brand of their Cosecha wine, and most of the Crianza and Reserva wines are bottled with the label La Montesa. The bodega also is known for Plácet, an excellent white wine made from Viura and aged in French oak barrels.

BODEGAS RAMÓN BILBAO

YEAR FOUNDED: 1924

Wines of note: Ramón Bilbao Crianza, Mirto

In the nineteenth century the Bilbao Murga family lived and grew grapes in Rioja Alta, and in 1924 Ramón Bilbao Murga opened a bodega in Haro. He was a pioneer in the practice of aging wines, and the bodega carrying his name remained in the family for three generations. After being converted to a corporation in 1972, the bodega was purchased in 1999 by the Zamora Group, one of the largest beverage conglomerates in Spain.

Although the bodega owns only 185 acres (75 hectares) in Rioja Alta, it buys fruit from many more acres cultivated by growers with whom it has worked for decades. Traditional styles of wine are bottled under the Ramón Bilbao label; they include a Crianza, a Reserva, and a Gran Reserva and a white wine fermented in oak. The Ramón Bilbao Viña Turzaballa Gran Reserva is made from 100 percent Tempranillo handpicked from seventy-five-year-old vines; it is made only in great vintages. In addition, Mirto is made from 100 percent Tempranillo and aged in French oak.

BODEGAS RIOJANAS

YEAR FOUNDED: 1890

Wines of note: Monte Real Reserva, Viña Albina Reserva
Viña Albina Semi-Dulce Blanco

Bodegas Riojanas is located along a tree-lined street in the historic wine village of Cenicero in the Najerilla Valley. Rafael Carreras Picó, a Catalan businessman, founded the great historic bodega, which features Gothic vaults and stone walls built by French experts who remained at the bodega until the early 1930s. After his death it was sold to brothers Román and Fortunato Artacho, and it is still run by family members, with the highly qualified and reserved Felipe Nalda Frías, the grandnephew of the brothers, now the winemaker. The family owns substantial vineyards in and around Cenicero.

The wines of Bodegas Riojanas are great classic Riojas. The bodega bottles wine under a variety of labels;

however, Monte Real is the most coveted brand, under which Reserva and Gran Reserva wines are made with 80 percent Tempranillo, 15 percent Mazuelo, and 5 percent Graciano grapes sourced from only the Monte Real vineyards. The other main label is Viña Albina, using grapes from various plots. In addition to a red Reserva and Gran Reserva, the portfolio includes some white wines of note, including an artisanal, barrel-fermented white and an elegant Viña Albina semidulce. Other wines are bottled with the label Puerta Vieja.

BODEGAS SIERRA CANTABRIA

YEAR FOUNDED: 1957

Wines of note: Sierra Cantabria Crianza, El Bosque

The respected Eguren family has been growing grapes in Rioja since 1870 and knows the land and the Tempranillo grape like few others. It was Don Guillermo Eguren who started this winery in 1957 in the very quaint village of San Vicente de la Sonsierra in Rioja Alta, and that original building is still in use. The bodega is named for the mountain range that protects the vineyards from the harsh Atlantic wind.

The winemaker for Sierra Cantabria plus three other bodegas is the confident and reserved Marcos Eguren, who took over the position in 1989. These properties are certainly the historic marker for his generation. All are on the left bank of the Ebro in Rioja Alta and Alavesa.

Almost all the wines are bottled as Sierra Cantabria, including a Crianza that is 98 percent Tempranillo and 2 percent Graciano. The grapes for the Reserva and Gran Reserva are picked from thirty-year-old vines. Finca El Bosque is made only from grapes grown on the parcel of 4 acres (1.6 hectares) planted by Guillermo Eguren more than fifty years ago. Other very limited production wines include El Puntido. The Organza barrel-fermented and aged white wine (see page 122) is made from the three white grape varieties of Rioja and represents a unique and rare tribute to the varieties.

BODEGAS VALDEMAR

YEAR FOUNDED: 1889

Wines of note: Inspiración Tempranillo Blanco, Inspiración Maturana Tinto, Conde de Valdemar Gran Reserva

The history of Bodegas Valdemar begins in 1899 with the Martínez Bujanda dynasty of Rioja winemaking, when Joaquín began the first winery in the village of Oyón in Rioja Alavesa. The family's business continued to expand, although its own name did not appear on a label until 1966. The bodega's current name has been in place since 2003, when it was changed to match that of its primary brand.

When Jesús Martínez Bujanda took over in 1945, the bodega had amassed 500 acres (210 hectares) of vines. He continued to add land until the late 1970s when he handed over the bodega to his three children, Jesús Junior, Carlos, and Pilar. The old bodega has been restored as a small museum, and a new winery made its first vintage in 1984.

The bodega follows Riojan tradition by mixing grapes from the three subregions; what differentiates it from others is that all the grapes are grown in vineyards it owns. Vineyards were bought in Rioja Baja in the 1980s, and other vines of both Tempranillo and Viura were purchased in Rioja Alta. The family now owns more than 1,000 acres (425 hectares).

The Conde de Valdemar label includes wines whose percentage of Tempranillo ranges from 85 percent to 90 percent. Also included in that brand is a 100 percent Viura barrel-fermented white as well as a rosé that is 85 percent Garnacha and 15 percent Tempranillo. The younger wines are bottled as Valdemar, and highly allocated bottles made from experimental grape varieties are labeled Inspiración Valdemar. They include a 100 percent Graciano wine.

BODEGAS DE VIÑEDOS DE ALDEANUEVA (CORTIJO)

YEAR FOUNDED: 1956

Wines of note: Cortijo Blanco, Cortijo Tinto

Located in Rioja Baja, this is one of the largest bodegas in all of Rioja, although its name may not be on the tip of consumers' tongues. The bodega is owned by a cooperative of 850 vineyard owners who own 6,395 acres (2,600 hectares) of land among them. This member ownership has an impact on both quality control and pricing, because there is no middleman. Only 50 percent of the acreage is Tempranillo; the remainder is made up of Garnacha, Graciano, Mazuelo, and Viura.

All the cooperative's wines are subzonal and are bottled with the bright orange Cortijo label, a word that means "small farm shack." All of the Cortijo wines are monovarietals. The red is 100 percent Tempranillo, the white is 100 percent Viura, and the rosé is 100 percent Garnacha.

LEFT: Bodegas Valdemar

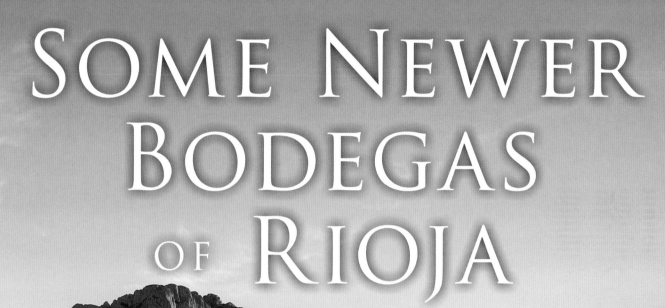

Some Newer Bodegas of Rioja

7

The range of wines produced by Rioja's bodegas becomes more exciting each year. This chapter covers wineries founded after 1960, although the DOCa Rioja experienced its fastest growth during the final fifteen years of the twentieth century. In 1983 there were 63 bodegas registered for aging, and by 2000 that number had grown to 222. This chapter presents only a sampling, with many more bodegas like these ready for wine professionals and wine lovers to explore.

Democracy took a deep breath in Spain in the last quarter of the twentieth century, and this was very evident in Rioja. Many of the bodegas started during that era were founded by people who had made their mark and earned their fortunes in other careers. As is the case in many wine regions around the world, they succumbed to the allure of owning a winery.

The numbers of Rioja wines have increased not only because of the creation of new bodegas but also because established bodegas have created new properties and added new wines to increase the stylistic variation of their existing labels. All the bodegas in this chapter export wines to North America, and at the end of the chapter there is a list of wines not currently available in that continent to keep in mind when traveling.

FINCA ALLENDE

YEAR FOUNDED: 1995

Wines of note: Finca Nueva Crianza, Calvario

The De Gregorio family has records showing that by the year 1800 its ancestors had been growing grapes in Rioja for a few centuries. In recent decades, Nicolás de Gregorio worked as a vineyard manager for Marqués de Murrieta; his son, Miguel Ángel de Gregorio, became the winemaker at Bodegas Bretón after completing his studies in Madrid. Miguel now runs Finca Allende along with his sister, Mercedes.

Allende is in historic Briones, in the Najerilla Valley in Rioja Alta, and the bodega released its first wine in 1995. Over time the family amassed ninety-two plots of grapes on the north and south sides of a hill; very low yields are a priority. The family's desire for a site-specific terroir is now reality.

CHAPTER OPENER: **Bodegas Ysios**
PREVIOUS PAGES: **Bodegas Murua**
PREVIOUS TOP RIGHT: **Bodegas Sierra Cantabria**
PREVIOUS BOTTOM RIGHT: **Bodegas López de Heredia**

Under the Finca Allende name are a Crianza made with 100 percent Tempranillo, a 100 percent Viura white wine, and a 100 percent Graciano wine. The flagship wines are Calvario, a single-vineyard Reserva made from vines planted in 1945, and Aurus, a single-vineyard Reserva made from 85 percent Tempranillo and 15 percent Graciano. Other labels are Finca Coronado, a high-expression wine, and Mártires, a barrel-fermented white wine.

ARTADI

YEAR FOUNDED: 1985

Wines of note: Viñas de Gain Crianza, Viña el Pison

Artadi began as a growers' cooperative when the highly regarded Juan Carlos López de la Calle persuaded some of his fellow grape growers in Rioja Alavesa to pool the grapes grown on their combined 175 acres (70 hectares) and make their own wines. Most of their wines are either single-estate or selected from very old vines, and the wines are made and aged, primarily in new French oak, in a building close to Laguardia.

The wines are very different because of the soil compositions in the Alavesa. Juan Carlos's grandfather first tended the pure chalk and limestone soil in which the Tempranillo grapes are planted for the Artadi Viña El Pison. Artadi Viñas de Gain and Pagos Viejos are the two main labels of this very low-production bodega. Artadi Grandes Añadas is produced only in exceptional vintages. In the tradition of the Alavesa, Artadi also has a carbonic maceration wine (see page 93) with a floral label.

BAIGORRI

YEAR FOUNDED: 2002

Wines of note: Baigorri Maceración Carbónica, Baigorri de Garage

Jesús Baigorri made his fortune in the travel industry and in 1997 decided to fulfill his dream of becoming a vintner. He hired Iñaki Aspiazu, a fellow Basque, as the architect for his winery, which sits high on a plateau in Rioja Alavesa, with spectacular views from inside. From the outside, all that is visible is a huge zinc and glass cube capped by a triangular roof. Not seen are the seven stories hidden underground, which allow the winery to use gravity in its processes. Other wineries use pumps to fill their stainless steel fermentation tanks; Baigorri uses only gravity to feed the wine into tanks as deep as six stories down. This bodega is one of the DOCa's best examples of functional architecture.

Baigorri's wine is as modern as the building. The wine is aged primarily in French oak complemented by some from Eastern Europe. The labels on all the bottles are essentially the same. The Crianza is a blend of Tempranillo and other grapes, and the Reserva is 100 percent Tempranillo from old vines. There is a Maceración Carbónica wine made from 100 percent Tempranillo as well as a barrel-fermented white wine aged in new French oak and a rosé that is a blend of Tempranillo and Garnacha. The flagship of the winery is the only wine that varies in name; it is Baigorri de Garage and is made from old vines.

BAI GORRI
DE GARAGE 2005

Wine processed with Tempranillo grapes picked manually one by one from very old, low production vines. Intense bigarreau cherry red color with aromas of fruit compote and hints of tobacco and liquorice. The oiliness provided by its tannins makes this an elegant, persistent wine.

R I O J A
DENOMINACION DE ORIGEN CALIFICADA

VISITING BODEGAS IN RIOJA

Most Americans are accustomed to "dropping in" on vineyards and their tasting rooms. In Rioja it is not that easy. Bodegas receive guests with quintessential Riojan hospitality, but only when they know you are coming; appointments need to be confirmed in advance.

This can be done on the various bodegas' websites, most of which are in Spanish and English. If you wish to visit a bodega that does not have an English site, use the translate button on your Web browser. Most bodegas do not charge for visits, although there are fees to try wines in the tasting rooms. Also, most are not open on Sundays and some close for the month of August.

When planning an itinerary, it makes sense to visit one subregion or one part of a subregion at a time. Travel within Rioja Alta can be up to forty-five minutes by car between points, and the same is true in Rioja Baja. Rioja Alavesa is a smaller area, and most villages are no more than fifteen minutes apart.

Unlike in many other wine regions of the world, many bodegas are located near or are in enchanting historic villages, some of which are highlighted in this book. Allow some extra time to get lost for a little while in these special places.

BARÓN DE LEY

YEAR FOUNDED: 1985

Wines of note: Reserva 7 Viñas, Barón de Ley Reserva

Monastic orders and the wine industry are a long and strong thread weaving through the tapestry of Rioja's history. Although the Barón de Ley bodega is relatively young, its home is a Benedictine monastery near the Navarese section of Rioja Baja that dates back to 1548. The Imas estate on the banks of the Ebro was home to the monks, their vineyards, and their sheep until 1836, when the order was ejected. It passed through many hands until a consortium of businessmen created a partnership with the government of Navarre to restore the monastery in return for permission to turn it into a winery.

The bodega then planted 220 acres (90 hectares) of vineyards to augment the old vines found on the site. The name of the bodega does not glorify a Spanish noble line; it means "lord of law" and was chosen to signal how the winemakers would treat the grapes. The owners of Barón de Ley also now owns El Coto (see page 189).

This is a single-estate property. The wines include 100 percent Tempranillo Reserva and rosé wines and a Gran Reserva that is 90 percent Tempranillo. The star of the line is the Finca Monasterio, a wine that is traditionally 80 percent Tempranillo, made from grapes picked in the old monastery garden in Mendavia, a village within the political boundaries of Navarre.

BODEGAS BERONIA

YEAR FOUNDED: 1973

Wines of note: Beronia Crianza, Beronia Gran Reserva

This Rioja Alta bodega, situated in the quaint village of Ollauri, is named for the original tribe that inhabited the lands of Rioja in the fifth century BCE, the Berones. Beronia was started by a consortium of Basque businessmen who enjoyed food and wine and decided they wanted their own bodega. Nine years later the famous sherry house González Byass purchased the bodega.

Beronia wines are truly great Modern Classic Riojas. Beronia owns 86 acres (35 hectares) of its own vineyards, and the vines on one 25-acre (10-hectare) plot are more than sixty years old. In addition, the bodega oversees production on more than 1,700 acres (700 hectares) owned by 150 separate owners—all within 10 miles (16 kilometers) of the winery itself.

All of the bodega's wines are bottled with the Beronia label, and in keeping with most Riojan bodegas, 95 percent of Beronia's wines are red. For the Crianza, Reserva, and Gran Reserva wines, the percentage of Tempranillo changes with the vintage. Rounding out the offerings are two 100 percent Viura white wines, one of which is barrel-aged, and a 100 percent Mazuelo red wine, one of the few in the region.

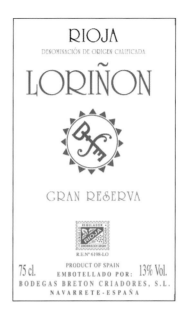

BODEGAS BRETÓN

YEAR FOUNDED: 1983

Wines of note: Alba de Bretón, Loriñón Gran Reserva

Started by Pedro Bretón Lasanta with financial backing from a group of businessmen in Logroño, this Rioja Alta bodega's first vintage was 1985, released in 1988. The bodega moved from Logroño to a new facility in Navarette, the center of the pottery industry in Rioja, in 2003 and today owns or controls 250 acres (100 hectares) of vineyard land, primarily in Agoncillo, Briones, and Ventosa. Its wines truly reflect the Modern Classic style.

Bodegas Bretón's wines are released under a panoply of names, most of which are linked to the names of its vineyards. One of the largest lines is Loriñón, which lists a Crianza, a Reserva, and a Gran Reserva consisting of 85 percent Tempranillo and a varying percentage of Graciano, Garnacha, and Mazuelo. Also in the line is a rosé that is 50 percent Tempranillo and 50 percent Garnacha as well as a barrel-fermented white wine. Domino de Conte is a single-estate Crianza, and Pagos del Camino is the bodega's 100 percent Garnacha wine. Alba de Bretón is a 100 percent Tempranillo wine, and Juvene, a recent addition, is a high-expression wine.

BODEGAS DARIEN

YEAR FOUNDED: 1999

Wines of note: Darien Reserva, Darien Selección

When the Riojan real estate mogul and businessman Luís Ilarraza founded the bodega in 1999, its name was Viñedos y Bodegas XXI, signifying the leap to a new century. In 2004, as has been the case with many properties, the name was changed to that of its leading brand as the bodega anticipated its move into a stunning modern building.

The bodega gleams like a beacon on the road from Logroño to Rioja Baja. Designed by J. Marino Pascual, the Logroño-based architect who designed the Dinastía Vivanco bodega and museum complex, the shimmering building looks like a piling up of the sheer cliffs and rock formations of Rioja.

The label on the Darien line is also modern, with a semicircle cut from the upper edge. The wines' names come from the arts: Georges Darien was a late nineteenth-century French writer, and the bodega's high-expression wine is named for the English composer Frederick

Delius. The rosé and Tempranillo are both 100 percent Tempranillo, and the composition of the Crianza and Reserva, aged in a combination of French and American oak, varies with the vintage. Two other wines—Darien Selección and Delius Reserva Especial—are produced in very small quantities. Both of these blends include the rescued varieties Mazuelo and Graciano, a nice touch from a modern property.

BODEGAS EL COTO

YEAR FOUNDED: 1970

Wines of note: El Coto Crianza, Coto Real Reserva

Though now part of the Barón de Ley Group (see page 186), Bodegas El Coto has been through a series of owners since its founding. The name comes from the Spanish word for "hunting estate," and the association is with the Coto de Imaz, a lodge in the Rioja Alavesa. This name appears on the bodega's Reserva and Gran Reserva wines.

The bodega is near Oyón in Rioja Alavesa and boasts a stunning octagonal tasting room. Winemaking is directed by the qualified Riojan native Luis Lucendo. The grapes are grown primarily in Cenicero in Rioja Alta, close to the Najerilla River, with additional grapes purchased from growers in the Alavesa.

Bottled as part of the El Coto brand, the label of which is dominated by a stunning buck, is a 100 percent

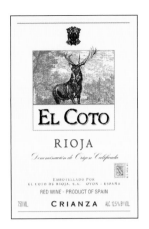

Tempranillo Crianza, a white wine of 100 percent Viura, and a rosé of 50 percent Tempranillo and 50 percent Garnacha. Both the Coto de Imaz Reserva and the Gran Reserva are 100 percent Tempranillo, and the Coto Real is 70 percent Tempranillo, 20 percent Garnacha, and 10 percent Graciano. El Coto wines are wonderful Modern Classic Riojas.

BODEGAS HEREDAD UGARTE

YEAR FOUNDED: 1989

Wines of note: Ugarte Cosecha, Heredad Ugarte Crianza

Descendants of the Eguren family were blessed with land and vineyards, but it took more than a century for the Ugarte branch of the family to make the switch from being grape growers in the San Vicente de Sonsierra section of Rioja Alavesa to being real vintners with a modern bodega in Laguardia. It was Don Amancio Ugarte's

BODEGAS LAN

YEAR FOUNDED: 1974

Wines of note: LAN Crianza, LAN Gran Reserva

grandson, Anastasio Jesús Eguren Ugarte, known as Victorino, who completed this important step in the family's history. He remains the titular head of the bodega and gives guidance to his daughters, Asunción and Mercedes, who now run the bodega day to day.

Their 296 acres (120 hectares) of vineyards are all in the Alavesa. Because of their history of land ownership they have access to Garnacha fruit, which has been increasingly difficult to obtain in Rioja. Garnacha is therefore part of their blends, something that is refreshing to see today. Their modern bodega building is built into a cliff with the aging cellars many feet below street level.

Heredad Ugarte has a large number of brands, including the Martín Cendoya label, named for Don Amancio's brother-in-law, a Reserva, and a Gran Reserva of mostly Tempranillo with some Graciano and Mazuelo. There is also a white wine made from 100 percent Malvasía grapes. Other labels for red wines are Dominio de Ugarte, Pagos de Eguren, Heredad Ugarte Crianza, Ugarte Cosecha, Condado de Eguren, and Anastasio.

This bodega's name is an acronym for Logroño, Álava, and Navarre. Situated in Rioja Alta near Fuenmayor, LAN produces wines by using the traditional Riojan model of buying grapes from many growers with whom it has long-established relationships. However, on the palate these wines are modern classics. They also produce single-vineyard wines with fruit from the Viña Lanciano plot of 180 acres (72 hectares); some of the vines in this vineyard are more than sixty years old. Much of the team at LAN is female, and the women of LAN are strong, qualified, and talented.

LAN makes only red wines, including a LAN Crianza that is 100 percent Tempranillo and a Reserva and Gran Reserva made from 80 percent Tempranillo, 10 percent Mazuelo, and 10 percent Garnacha. Viña Lanciano Reserva, Culmen Reserva, and LAN Edición Limitada are all single-vineyard wines; the latter two are made from old vines in the Pago El Rincón section of the vineyards.

BODEGAS MARQUÉS DE CÁCERES (UNIÓN VITIVINÍCOLA)

YEAR FOUNDED: 1970

Wines of note: Marqués de Cáceres Crianza, Marqués de Cáceres Reserva, MC

Enrique Forner's family was originally from Valencia and was in the wine business there. But when he decided where to settle after a self-imposed exile in Bordeaux during the Spanish Civil War, the choice was Cenicero, a village in Rioja Alta. There he built a winery clearly indebted to the French château style, with imposing iron gates.

The title in the name of the bodega is actually borrowed. It was originally granted in the eighteenth century to Juan Ambrosio García de Cáceres y Montemayor, a captain of the Royal Armada. His heirs allowed the Forner family to use their title as the bodega's name.

The late Forner asked his French mentor, the famed enologist Émile Peynaud, to serve as adviser for the venture. Their first vintage was released in 1975. Since that time Marqués de Cáceres has earned much reverence for its wines, professionalism, and contributions to Rioja.

The bodega bottles most of its wines under the Marqués de Cáceres label, including a red Crianza, Reserva, and Gran Reserva; a rosé; and a white wine. But other labels have joined the ranks. MC, a high-expression wine made with 100 percent Tempranillo, is a recent addition, and Gaudium was added in 1994. The name is the Latin word for "joy" and it is made only in extremely good years with grapes from very old vines. Recently introduced white wines are Satinela, a lovely semidulce made from grapes harvested late, once their sugar had concentrated, and Antea, a barrel-fermented white.

BODEGAS MURIEL

YEAR FOUNDED: 1986

Wines of note: Muriel Crianza, JME

Bodegas Muriel, located in Elciego in Rioja Alavesa, has far more history than its founding date would imply. This is actually the rebirth of a bodega that was started in 1926 by Don José Murúa Villaverdo, who came from a long line of winemakers. Julián Murúa Train resurrected the winery, which still contained wines produced by his parents. The name Bodegas Muriel is a combination of his name, Murúa, and Elciego, the town where the bodega is located.

A full line of 100 percent Tempranillo wines is bottled under the Muriel label. They include a Crianza, a Reserva, and a Gran Reserva aged in a combination of French and American oak. Also under that label are a rosé of 50 percent Tempranillo and 50 percent Garnacha and a white wine of 100 percent Viura. JME is the label on the bodega's high-expression wine.

NUESTRA SEÑORA DE REMELLURI

YEAR FOUNDED: 1967

Wines of note: Remelluri Blanco, Remelluri Reserva

Rioja is rich with history, and perhaps no spot reflects this more than the area around Nuestra Señora de Remelluri. A necropolis from the late Middle Ages is at this location outside of Labastida in Rioja Alavesa, as

well as the ruins of the Toloño monastery, dating from the fourteenth century. Hugging the Toloño mountain range are the earliest traces of the wine business in Rioja, with records in the town hall of Labastida dating back to 1596. There is a small museum at the bodega with many fascinating artifacts that span centuries.

In 1967, the Basque industrialist Jaime Rodríguez Salis purchased the farm and began restoring all the old vineyard lands. In the 1980s his son, Telmo Rodríquez, who was trained in France, came to the winery and brought with him skill, talent, and bold new perspectives. The bodega now has more than 275 acres (112 hectares) under cultivation and was one of the first bodegas in Rioja to bottle single-estate wines. Today Telmo Rodríguez directs other fascinating projects in Rioja and in other DO regions of Spain.

The Remelluri Reserva is made from 90 percent Tempranillo, 5 percent Graciano, and 5 percent Garnacha. The most touted red wine is the Colección Jaime Rodríguez Reserva, and there is another wine labeled La Granja Remelluri. The bodega also produces a white wine under the Remelluri label.

BODEGAS ONTAÑÓN

YEAR FOUNDED: 1984

Wines of note: Arteso, Ontañón Reserva

Founded by Gabriel Pérez Marzo and now run by his son and daughter, Rubén and Raquel, Ontañon is one of the principal bodegas waving the flag for Rioja Baja.

On Bodegas Ontañón's website, three phrases are given equal importance: "Passion for Vines. Passion for Wine. Passion for Art." This motto is certainly reflected in its bodega cum art gallery on the outskirts of Logroño. Grapes come from the more than 600 acres (250 hectares) owned by the family in Rioja Baja. One of its landmark vineyards is La Montesa on the slopes of the Yerga Mountains at the highest altitude in which grapes will grow; another is in the village of Quel. All the vineyards are located in the Cidacos and Alhama valleys of Rioja Baja.

A Crianza, a Reserva, and a Gran Reserva, the latter two composed of 95 percent Tempranillo and 5 percent Graciano, are bottled with the Ontañón label. Collección Mitológica is the name given to the bodega's Gran Reserva wine, and Arteso is the label of its young wines.

A MODERN MUSEUM OF MYTHOLOGY

Bodegas Ontañón's art collection, which is displayed throughout a converted candy factory on the outskirts of Logroño, contains sculptures, stained glass windows, and paintings by one artist, Miguel Ángel Sáinz. Regardless of the medium, the works relate to Greek and Roman mythology. A Rioja native and an accomplished sculptor and artist, Sáinz paired his art degrees from Madrid with studies at the theological seminary in Logroño and was regarded as a highly spiritual person. He was a close friend of Gabriel Pérez, and the bodega truly represents their partnership and mutual reverence. Each of the aging cellars on this site contains oversized sculptures, and aesthetic touches are found at every turn in the functional building. Many of Sáinz's works can also be found in public places throughout La Rioja.

BODEGAS TOBÍA

YEAR FOUNDED: 1994

Wines of note: Alma de Tobía Rosado,
Tobía Graciano, Tobía Reserva

Bodegas Tobía is the result of the vision and drive of one
man, Óscar Tobía. The bodega is located in the enchanting village of Cuzcurrita del Río Tirón in the "Alta Alta,"
the northwesternmost area of Rioja Alta.

Óscar embodies the essence of twenty-first-century
Rioja. He is the son of a family of Riojan grape growers
from San Asensio and chose the challenging road to move
forward and make his own wine. He studied enology at
the University of Valencia and did postgraduate work at
the University of Rioja. Óscar is restless and passionate
about expressing the ultimate diversity and complexity of
Rioja, and this spirit is reflected in his wines. The winery

does not own vineyards but harvests grapes from fifteen
plots that together constitute a total of 200 acres
(80 hectares) throughout the DOCa.

Highlights of this interesting portfolio are an unusual
and exciting barrel-fermented rosé labeled Alma de Tobía,
the Alma de Tobía barrel-fermented white wine, a
100 percent Graciano, and the Tobía line of red wines.

REMÍREZ DE GANUZA

YEAR FOUNDED: 1988

Wines of note: Remírez de Ganuza Reserva,
Remírez de Ganuza Gran Reserva, Transnocho

Fernando Remírez de Ganuza was born in Navarre but
considers Rioja Alavesa his true home. After many years
of owning both vineyards and interests in wineries, he

decided he wanted his own, and his first vintage was released in 1991. Fernando knows the vineyards of the DOCa Rioja like very few people. He designed the winery and lovingly had an ancient building moved stone by stone to the beautiful village of Samaniego. He now owns 160 acres (65 hectares) of vineyards in the Alavesa villages of Samaniego, Laguardia, Leza, and Elciego.

This bodega juxtaposes tradition and innovation. It is new, yet some of the techniques Remírez de Ganuza is employing are centuries old; one example is *cepillado de las cepas* (brushing of the vines). This labor-intensive practice involves removing dried strips of bark from the vines as a way to reduce the risk of infestation. Some of his other techniques border on revolutionary. He determined that because bunches of grapes are wider at the top, the fruit on the top becomes riper than that at the pointed tip. In his winery the tips are cut off and sent to a vat below to become a young wine produced by carbonic maceration (see page 93). Most of the oak he uses is American, with the remainder French and East European, and he decides with each vintage what proportion of each type to use.

The bodega issues a Remírez de Ganuza Reserva and Gran Reserva. Other wines are labeled Erre Punto, with the appropriate "R." dominating the bottle. These include a barrel-fermented white wine and the carbonic maceration red wine. His flagship wine is the Transnocho.

BODEGAS RODA

YEAR FOUNDED: 1987

Wines of note: RODA I Reserva, Cirsion

When Catalán natives Mario Rottlant and his wife, Carmen Daurella, decided to become vintners in Rioja, they were already experienced in the world of fine food and wine from allied businesses. With Rioja Alta as their subregion, their goal was to create modern-style wines using the traditional grape varieties. The name RODA was formed by joining the first two letters of their last names.

The couple worked with the highly revered current winemaker and poet Agustín Santolaya, who knew every square foot of land in the region, to purchase vineyards. They took a risk with the purchase of a 150-acre (60-hectare) estate with no extant planting in a region in which the age of vines is frequently touted.

They then developed relationships with growers in both Rioja Alta and Rioja Baja whose vines were more than thirty years old.

It was seven years after the founding of the bodega that any wine appeared under its label; the managing team had determined that if it was not up to their standards, it would be sold in bulk. According to news articles, there was an eager market for the unwanted wine.

RODA now has four labels. RODA I is the line of firmer, more structured wines, and RODA (formerly called RODA II) is the label for the more high-expression wines; both account for slightly less than 50 percent of the bottling. Cirsion, started in 1998, is made from grapes vinified from select clusters from various plots at the very end of the ripening period. This is the sort of intellectual process that RODA brings to its wines. The latest addition is SELA, a young wine made from 96 percent Tempranillo and 4 percent Graciano.

TORRES

YEAR FOUNDED: 2006

Wines of note: Ibéricos

Torres is a great name not only in Spain but in the world of wine; it is synonymous with Spanish wine history. This legendary family firm was founded in 1870 and by the end of the twentieth century had wineries not only in Spain but also in California and Chile and a joint venture in China. After going global, the company looked at DO regions in Spain and chose Rioja and Priorat for expansion.

They purchased land in Rioja Alavesa in 2005, and the first wine was released in 2007. Consistent with the Torres family philosophy, the bodega, situated in Labastida, was designed to be as green as possible, and it will become even more so in years to come. The complex was designed by the Catalan architect Gabriel Barba. The initial construction phase included a reservoir to collect rainwater as well as a treatment plant to process it; in 2011 solar panels were scheduled to be installed on the roof.

For now, the only label is Ibéricos, which carries a Crianza age label although the winery presents it as an iconic wine. It is a monovarietal Tempranillo from grapes grown in the Alavesa. Although Riojan in style, this bold, confident wine undoubtedly has the Torres family signature in the nose and on the palate. The wine is aged in both French and American oak barrels, some of them new. This is a great example of a subzonal Rioja.

FINCA VALPIEDRA

YEAR FOUNDED: 1999

Wines of note: Cantos de Valpiedra Cosecha, Finca Valpiedra Reserva

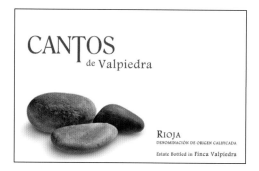

Impeccable and exquisite inside and out, this estate is located in a beautifully picturesque setting on the banks of the Ebro River. Finca Valpiedra is a single-estate property owned by the Martínez Bujanda family, which purchased the land more than thirty years ago with the goal of making single-estate wines. The vineyard is in the Najerilla Valley of Rioja Alta on an extraordinary bend of the Ebro River between the villages of Cenicero and Fuenmayor. The 198-acre (80-hectare) vineyard is divided into nine plots. The property and attention to winemaking represent the meticulous care and traits of the Martinez Bujanda family.

The main wine, Finca Valpiedra Reserva, is primarily Tempranillo but can contain small amounts of Graciano; the wine is aged only in new French oak. There is also Cantos de Valpiedra, which is a 100 percent Tempranillo Cosecha aged 70 percent in French oak and 30 percent in American oak.

BODEGAS VALSACRO

YEAR FOUNDED: 1997

Wines of note: Valsacro Crianza, Arvum

In a departure from the common practice in Rioja of expanding a bodega or buying another one, Amador and Jesús Escudero decided to close their family's four-generation-old facility in Rioja Baja and start again, this time with an estate-style winery in the French tradition. Although their father, Benito Escudero, had modernized

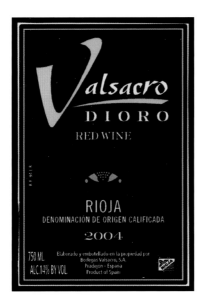

BODEGAS VIÑA IJALBA

YEAR FOUNDED: 1975

Wines of note: Ijalba Graciano, Ijalba Reserva

Bodegas Escudero significantly in the early 1990s, the pair launched Bodegas Valsacro in 1997 and released its first wine in 2001. Amador, who was trained in Bordeaux, is the winemaker, and his brother is the viticulturist. Both the family and its wines embody the history, vineyards, and potential of Rioja Baja.

Today, huge stainless steel fermentation vats share a cavernous hall with barrels of wine aging in oak. The Valsacro vineyards range in age from fairly new to more than eighty years old and are owned primarily by the family.

The wines are bottled primarily under the Valsacro name. The Crianza is 50 percent Tempranillo, 40 percent Garnacha, and 10 percent Mazuelo aged in a combination of French and American oak. At the next level is Valsacro Dioro, made from carefully selected grapes and given aging in new French oak. Razón is a high-expression wine.

The preparation for Viña Ijalba began in 1975 when Dionisio Ruiz Ijalba, who was in the business of extracting gravel in Rioja Alta, decided to fill the resulting holes with soil and begin planting grapes. For fifteen years he sold the grapes to other bodegas. In 1991 he built a state-of-the-art bodega in the Iregua Valley that is certified by the Common Market for sustainable construction and operation. The bodega now has 198 acres (80 hectares) of vineyards near Logroño, in San Vicente de Sonsierra, and in the Oja valley.

The bottle used by Bodegas Viña Ijalba is tall and sleek, approximately three inches taller than the classic "Bordeaux bottle" used by most Rioja wineries. The tinted glass has anti-ultraviolet light properties to keep light from damaging the wine.

Ijalba labels a Crianza of 90 percent Tempranillo and 10 percent Graciano, a Reserva with the same formulation, and a Selección Especial, made only in excellent years, that is 50 percent Tempranillo and 50 percent Graciano. There is also a 100 percent Graciano wine, which, when it was first released in 1995, was the first all-Graciano in the DOCa Rioja. The Dionisio Ruiz Ijalba is 100 percent Maturana Tinta, and the Genoli label is used on bottles of 100 percent Maturana Blanca. Much more typical of the Alavesa than of Rioja Alta, Solferino is the brand of wine produced by carbonic maceration (see page 93).

BODEGAS Y VIÑEDOS LABASTIDA

YEAR FOUNDED: 1964

Wines of note: Labastida Crianza, Manuel de Quintano Reserva

The Unión de Cosecheros de Labastida, the legal entity that owns this bodega, is a cooperative of more than 125 vintners in Rioja Alavesa; it is the largest cooperative winery in the Basque Country. Those vintners control 1,330 acres (540 hectares) of vineyards with vines more than twenty-five years old dispersed in 1,063 plots with an average size of 0.5 hectare, which exactly mirrors the average plot size in the DOCa.

During the era of late Francoism, these men were authentic pioneers and visionaries in their ability to see the potential in Rioja wine and begin to form a private sector. Now, fifty years later, a truly intergenerational team spirit lives and thrives here. The second generation of families runs the cooperative and supervises every element from pruning the vines to blending the grapes. The very talented winemaker, Manuel Ruiz Pedreira, is the son of a highly regarded historian and enologist in Rioja, Manuel Ruiz Hernández.

The bodega's wines are all subzonal and are bottled under different labels. Solagüen, named for a vineyard, is the label on one line of wines. Another is Castillo Labastida, which includes a new and solid Cosecha Madurado, Crianza, and rosé made with 100 percent Tempranillo. Solagüen Cepas Viejas is 62 percent Tempranillo and 38 percent Garnacha, and there is also a worthy fruit-forward white. Another is the Manuel Quintano, named for the famed theologian who brought the concept of aging wines to Rioja (see page 147), Appropriately, the Quintano label is used only on Reserva and Gran Reserva wines.

BODEGAS YSIOS

YEAR FOUNDED: 2001

Wines of note: Ysios Reserva,
Ysios Reserva Edición Limitada

The name of this bodega comes from a combination of the names of two Egyptian gods, Isis and Osiris; Isis was the goddess of magic who oversaw the conversion of grapes into wine, and Osiris was her brother and later husband, who was the first king of the earth. Any gods would be honored to be feted in a palace like this one on the out-skirts of Laguardia in Rioja Alavesa. From the entry gates to Laguardia the bodega appears to sit like a shawl draped on a chair.

Vineyards, primarily planted with Tempranillo vines that are between twenty-five and thirty years old, surround Ysios. The winemaker is Luis Zudaire, who graduated from the University of Montpellier in France and worked in France as well as in Chile and Argentina before returning to Rioja.

Almost all wines bottled at Ysios bear this name and a drawing of the roofline of the bodega on the labels, and all are 100 percent Tempranillo. The line includes a Reserva and a Reserva Edición Limitada, the grapes for which are picked from a vineyard named Las Navas in El Villar that is eighty years old; it is produced only in exceptional vintages, and each of the 5,000 bottles is numbered. Esencia de Ysios and Ysios & Ion Fiz are more high-expression wines.

AN ARCHITECTURAL ECHO

Even tourists with no interest in wine flock to see the Bodegas Ysios building, which was designed by the internationally famous and award-winning architect Santiago Calatrava. This brilliant architect of twenty-first-century Spain is a native of Valencia and now has offices around the world.

The winery's undulating roof, made from a series of laminated wooden beams, both resembles a row of barrels and mirrors the curves of the mountains behind it. In both color and shape, the bodega is set before the peaks of the Sierra de Cantabria Mountains, which echo its form.

A SAMPLING OF MORE GREAT WINES

Rioja's bodegas all deserve a listing in this book, but space does not permit it. Here are some wines that are highly recommended and are available in North America. They are divided by style categories and are listed by wine name and bodega

WHITE WINES

Benito Urbina Blanco / Bodegas Benito Urbina

Esencias de Varal / Bodegas Varal

Izadi White / Bodegas Izadi

Leza García / Bodegas Leza García

Ostatu Blanco / Bodegas Ostatu

Predicador Blanco / Benjamin Romeo

Rinsol / Bodegas Franco Españolas

Tempranillo Blanco-Ad Libitum /
  Juan Carlos Sancha

Vallobera Blanco / Bodegas Vallobera

WHITE WINES WITH A HINT OF OAK

B de Basilio / Bodegas Águila Real

Becquer / Bodegas Escudero

Brozal Blanco / Bodegas El Indiano

Finca Nueva Blanco / Finca Nueva

Reserva Blanco / Casado Morales

Ruiz de Viñaspre Blanc / Bodegas Ruiz de Viñaspre

Viña Valoria Crianza / Viña Valoria

ROSÉS

El Circulo Rosado / Pagos del Rey

Ermita de San Felices Rosado / Bodegas Santalba

Santurnia / Bodegas Ramón Ayala Lete e Hijos

COSECHAS (YOUNG WINES)

Arbanta / Biurko Gorri

Calma / Don Sancho Londoño

Campellares / Bodegas San Pedro Apóstol

Deobriga / Bodegas Ramón Ayala Lete e Hijos

Gran Familia / Castello de Fuenmayor

Mencos / Manso de Zúñiga

Montebuena / Bodegas Montebuena

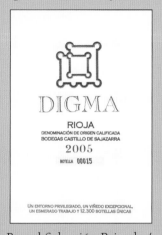

Ramón Cordova Cosecha /
  Bodegas Ramón Cordova

Riba Guda Cosecha / Bodegas Fin de Siglo

Rioja Vega / Rioja Vega

Solar de Randez / Bodegas Las Orcas

Solnia / Bodegas y Viñedos Ilurce

Tendencia / Bodega San Prudencio Rioja Cueto

Viña Herminia / Bodegas Viña Herminia

HIGH-EXPRESSION (NEW WAVE) COSECHAS

Aduna-Vendimia Seleccionada /
  Bodegas Heredad Aduna

AUDIUS / Antiguas Viñas de Rioja

B de Basilio / Bodegas Águila Real

Contador / Benjamín Romeo

Deobriga 2004 /
  Bodegas Ramón de Ayala Lete e Hijos

Digma / Bodegas Castillo de Sajazarra

Dominio de Berzal Selección Privada /
  Domino de Berzal

Egomei/ Finca Egomei

Ganko / Oliveir Riviere

La Orbe / Martínez Laorden

LZ / Compañia de Vinos de Telmo Rodríguez

Malpuesto / Bodegas Orben

Orgullo / Bodegas Orgullo

Picea 650 / Viñedos del Ternero

Pujanza Norte / Bodegas y Viñedos Pujanza

XdT / XdT

CRIANZAS

Altos Crianza / Altos de Rioja

Barón Ladrón de Guevara Crianza /
    Bodegas Valdelana

Belezos Crianza/Bodegas Zugobar

Biga / Luberri

Domino de Berzal Crianza/Domino de Berzal

Lagar de Santiago Crianza / Bodegas de Santiago

Lealtanza Crianza / Bodegas Altanza

Magister Bibendi Crianza / Navarrsotillo

Marqués de la Vitoria Crianza /
    Bodegas Marqués de la Victoria

Medrano Crianza / Bodegas Medrano Irazu

Mencos Crianza / Manso de Zúñiga

Miranda Crianza / Viñedos de Ternero

Obalo Crianza / Bodegas Obalo

Olarra Añares Crianza / Bodegas Olarra

Ondalan Crianza / Bodegas Ondalan

Osoti / Bodegas Osoti

Ostatu Crianza / Bodegas Ostatu

Rincón de Navas 2005 / Bodegas Valgrande

Rondan Crianza / Bodegas Sáenz de Santamaría

Señorio de P. Peciña Crianza /
    Bodegas Hermanos Peciña

Urbion Crianza / Bodegas Vinícola Real

Viña Olagosa Crianza / Bodegas Perica

Zinio Crianza / Bodegas Patrocinio

Zuazo Gaston Crianza / Bodegas Zuazo Gaston

VALUE CRIANZAS

Covila Crianza / Bodegas Covila

CUETO / Bodegas San Prudencio

Cuna de Reyes Crianza / Bodegas Cuna de Reyes

Marqués de Arienzo Crianza / Bodegas Domecq

Marqués de Tomares /
   Bodegas Marqués de Tomares

Pinturas Crianza / Pinturas

Rincón de Navas Crianza / Bodegas Valgrande

Señorio de Labarta Crianza / Viñedos de Labarta

Solar de Samaniego Crianza / Bodegas Alavesas

Vaza Crianza / Solar Viejo

Viña Berceo Crianza / Grupo Berceo

Viña Herminia Crianza / Bodegas Viña Herminia

RESERVAS

Aduna Reserva / Bodegas Heredad de Aduna

Arviza Reserva / Bodegas Marqués de Arviza

Aspaldi Reserva / Bodegas Aspaldi

Barón de Oña Reserva / Torre de Oña

Bordón Reserva / Bodegas Franco Españolas

Castillo de Cuzcurrita Reserva /
   Señorío Castillo de Cuzcurrita

Cerro Añon Reserva / Bodegas Olarra

Conde de la Salceda Reserva / Viña Salceda

Edulis Reserva / Bodegas Altanza

Hacienda López de Haro / Bodegas Clássica

Heras Cordón Vendimia Selecciona /
   Bodegas y Viñedos Heras Cordón

Marqués de Terán Reserva /
   Bodegas Regalía de Ollauri

Marqués de Vargas Reserva /
   Bodegas Marqués de Vargas

Miguel Merino Reserva / Bodegas Miguel Merino

Muro Reserva / Bodegas Miguel Ángel Muro

Ondarre Mayor Reserva / Bodegas Ondarre

Rentas de Fincas R 2002 / Bodegas Mateos

Reserva Valenciso 2004 / Bodegas Valenciso

Siglo Reserva / Bodegas AGE

Solabel Reserva / Bodegas Solabel

Solar de Randez 2001 / Bodegas Las Orcas

Urbina Reserva Especial / Bodegas Benito Urbina

Valserrano Reserva 2004 /
    Bodegas y Vinos de la Marquésa

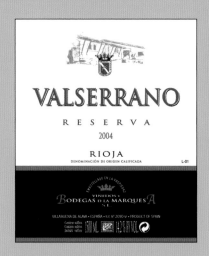

GRAN RESERVAS

Campillo Gran Reserva 1994 / Bodegas Campillo

Diez-Caballero Gran Reserva / Diez-Caballero

Ramírez de la Piscina Gran Reserva /
    Bodegas Ramírez de la Piscina

Valserrano Gran Reserva / Bodegas de la Marquesa

WINES TO TRY WHEN TRAVELING

All the bodegas profiled in Chapters 6 and 7 have distribution in North America. Even if you cannot find these wines at your favorite shop, with some sleuthing on the Internet you will be able to try them. Here is a list of select bodegas whose wines are not available in the United States at the time of this writing but are recommended if you see them in shops or on restaurant lists while abroad in Spain or in other countries to which they are exported.

Bodegas Alicia Rojas

Bodegas Ciego del Rey

Bodegas Corral

Bodegas David Moreno

Bodegas El Cidacos

Bodegas Fernández de Pierola

Bodegas Fuenmayor

Bodegas Loli Casado

Bodegas Puelles

Bodegas y Viñedos Tobelos

Bodegas y Viñedos Gómez Cruzado

Finca de los Arandinos

Viñedos Ruiz Jiménez

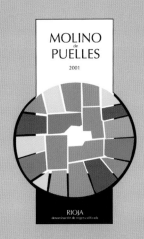

RIOJA
ON THE
MODERN
TABLE

8

Riojan tradition celebrates the pleasures of life, and what could be more central to this theme than great wines and great food? But in Rioja it goes further; it also includes the sacred privilege of sharing a table with friends, family, colleagues, or even strangers. In the last few decades this tradition has been forming a strong root system in North America too.

As the quality of food has escalated on this continent, so have the options for more diverse ethnic dining. We live in an era in which there is a veritable United Nations of Cuisines in almost every city and even in some small towns. Not only are supermarkets filled with a wide variety of fruits, vegetables, and every other food imaginable, there are more cookbooks available offering instruction on how to handle the bounty. And it's wonderful that the wine of the Tempranillo grape goes with all of them.

Rioja wine is truly "cuisine compatible." It doesn't have the lip-pursing tannins of some wines or their alienating high level of alcohol. Red Riojas even when young have a balance of flavors that enhances a wide array of foods as well as methods of preparation. Rioja can be a perfect mate to a pepperoni pizza one night and a grilled salmon the next. What makes Rioja such a good partner with foods is its harmonic balance of fruit and acidity, its flavorful spectrum of red berry fruit, and its soft tannins.

PAIRING FOOD WITH RIOJA

Rioja wines are voluptuous; they are round and full and rich. They are not Audrey Hepburn; they are more Marilyn Monroe. For this reason, they pair with myriad foods, some of which are typical of most red wines and some of which would be paired with white wines in other books. The soft tannins in Rioja are strong enough to cleanse the palate, but then the fruit enters the picture and can calm even a high level of spice.

The traditional advice has been that you should drink wines from the same land that produced the food, but that is not a hard and fast rule. You should drink wines that make your food taste even better, and Rioja is one of those wines. Admittedly, Rioja is not the wine for every dish. Shellfish, such as raw oysters, and fish or poultry cooked in cream sauce would not be compatible with Rioja. But those are the exceptions rather than the rule.

Here are some categories of foods that pair well with Rioja:

- **ANYTHING GRILLED.** The fruit in the wine, especially the berry notes, balances the smoky nuances of food coming from the grill. This can be anything from slices of eggplant to a salmon steak, with all red meats included. A classic Rioja, which often includes grape varieties other than Tempranillo, adds woodsy and earthy nuances; a modern classic Crianza is also a good choice.

• **ANYTHING MADE WITH VIBRANT SPICES OR PEPPERS.** Although delicate herbs such as tarragon and chervil might work well with a grassy Sauvignon Blanc, the panoply of spices used in Hispanic, Middle Eastern, and Indian food works wonderfully with Rioja. The fruit in Rioja softens spices such as cumin, coriander, harissa, curry, cilantro, paprika, cinnamon, and turmeric. The bright berry fruit of a number of 100 percent Tempranillo rosés today is a great, unique choice for many Mexican dishes. Middle Eastern foods would be celestial with a Maturana Tinta (a rare find that requires perseverance), but a great alternative would be a subzonal Crianza from Rioja Baja, where very often the Tempranillo fruit is riper than that of the other two subregions.

• **ASIAN FOOD.** For the last few decades the common wisdom among wine writers was that Asian food should be served with white wines, but that is hardly the only alternative, especially with meat dishes. Ingredients such as fresh ginger, toasted sesame oil, star anise and five-spice powder, hoisin sauce, and salty sauces such as soy sauce and fish sauce all work well with Rioja, which mellows and softens their savory profile. A fruit-forward white is also a good choice, and many white Riojas containing Malvasía would work here.

• **ANYTHING IN A TOMATO SAUCE.** This can be Italian, Spanish, or North American, but if it has a tomato sauce, it works with Rioja, whether poultry, meat, fish, or vegetarian. It can be spicy or mild, pasta sauce or pizza. Fruit goes with fruit, and tomato, as an acidic fruit, is balanced and sweetened by the berry nuances in Rioja. Depending on the dish, there is a wide range of options here, but based on aging levels, a Cosecha, Crianza, or Reserva is the way to go.

• **ROASTED POULTRY.** There is nothing more perfect than a roast chicken seasoned with a mixture of herbs and garlic coming from the oven, and the lightness of Rioja works with the white meat, whereas the richness of the dark meat is enhanced by the soft tannins. Modern Classic single-vineyard or single-estate wines work well with poultry.

• **GAME BIRDS.** In Spain's mountainous terrain, small game thrives; there is very little space for cattle to graze. Duck, quail, partridge, and guinea hen all have a strong, gamy note to their flavor. These are the native foods of Rioja, and traditional and classic Riojas are perfect choices.

• **FINFISH DISHES.** Delicate sole is enhanced by the subtle fruit of the Viura grape in a white Rioja, but any "meaty" fish, such as swordfish, salmon, or tuna, can stand up to a red Rioja. A modern classic Cosecha or Crianza would pair well.

• **ANY RED MEAT, REGARDLESS OF THE PREPARATION METHOD.** This is the most obvious of the pairing profiles, which is why it is last on the list. Of course Rioja marries with all red meats, but this is where the degree of aging enters the picture. More vibrantly seasoned dishes can be served with younger wines, whereas a very simple dish such as a grilled steak or roasted leg of lamb will bring out the subtle nuances in a Reserva or Gran Reserva. High-expression Riojas pair well with the fattier meats, but in general a Reserva or Gran Reserva is compatible too.

CHEESE MATCHES

A few wedges of cheese with some crusty bread or crackers can complement a tapas spread or start or end a meal; there are many Riojas that are great partners with cheese, and many of them are white.

All cheese is created when bacterial cultures—either found naturally in the animal's milk or added if the milk has been pasteurized—produce acid and thus sour the milk. The resulting curd is salted, heated, and formed into its final shape. Cow, goat, and ewe milk all evolve differently.

When the acid in the maturing process creates a hard cheese with nutty, sharp, and salty flavors such as Manchego, Parmesan, or Comté, it goes well with all red wines, especially Rioja, because the soft tannins bring out the subtler flavors in the cheese. A high-expression Rioja would work well, as would a complexly layered Gran Reserva. A white Rioja has the acidity to cut through the creaminess of soft cheeses such as Brie, and the fruit in a rosé highlights the sweetness of creamy cheeses. The degree of oak in the wine can influence the pairing, and advice from a helpful merchant may be welcome here.

Cheese and wine are similar foods because each changes significantly as it ages, but the aging process works in diametrically opposite ways. In the case of wine, aging creates complexity and nuance, whereas in the case of cheese, the evaporation of liquid hardens the texture as the work of bacteria intensifies the flavor.

A young cheese such as Havarti works well with a Crianza, whereas aged Gouda or aged cheddar is the cheese to serve with a Reserva or Gran Reserva. Avoid serving red wine with blue-veined cheeses such as Stilton and Gorgonzola, but the semidulce white Riojas are a great choice. Serve some dried fruit such as apricots or quince paste along with the cheeses to add more sweetness to the plate.

SOME RECIPES FROM RIOJA

Just as the architecture in Rioja juxtaposes classic buildings with the excitement of those designed in the twenty-first century, the same can be said for the food. There is a wonderful range of restaurants in Rioja, from traditional to modern, all using the superb produce and other foods of the region. Uniting these disparate dishes are the wines of the region.

This chapter includes some of the best recipes from two award-winning chefs in Rioja: Lorenzo Cañas and Francis Paniego. They are a generation apart, but both are dedicated to excellence.

LORENZO CAÑAS: THE FATHER OF RIOJAN CUISINE

Lorenzo Cañas is unquestionably revered by many generations of Riojans as the father of Riojan cuisine. Born in a humble neighborhood in Logroño in 1947, he is a self-made man whose passion for Rioja and its crops has fueled his success.

When he receives visitors at his palatial event-only restaurant, La Merced, it is in a sitting room and office suite with walls lined from chair rail to vaulted ceiling with memorabilia and awards. There he is in a photo with the king and queen of Spain. Nearby is a certificate for the years he served as president of La Asociación Española de Restaurantes de Buena Mesa (the Spanish Association of Restaurants of the Good Table), the oldest such professional organization in the country. Below it is an award he cherishes; in 2005 the government of La Rioja gave him the title of Riojano Ilustre, the highest civilian honor that it can bestow.

This is not a vanity wall regardless of the fact that his tally of medals surpasses that of a five-star general. It is testimony to this energetic man, whose hair is as sparkling white as his apron and jacket. He is so respected by his peers that Juan Mari Arzak, the multistarred Michelin chef from San Sebastián, did not hesitate to speak his name when asked which Spanish chef he most admired. In 1979, when Paul Bocuse was hired to cook a celebratory meal for a Riojan bodega, he

saw that Lorenzo Cañas was also participating at the event. "Why did they hire me when they have you here?" he said to the Spanish chef.

As was the case for many of his generation, Cañas studied in kitchens throughout Spain; in 1971, at the tender age of twenty-four, he opened his first restaurant, a traditional Riojan *mesón*. That was followed in 1983 by the first La Merced, located in the Old Quarter of Logroño. Critics flocked to sample his cooking, but the restaurant was ahead of its time for Rioja in that era, and it closed.

In 1999 he transferred the name to his present site, a cavernous banquet hall with a commanding view of vineyards that seats up to 1,200. Its huge kitchen—which is as pristine as an operating room—is divided into zones. In one cubicle a chef fillets fish, saving the skeletons for a crew around the corner making stocks. In another room, cooks, including his daughter Elia, are meticulously and artfully arranging presentation platters of sausages to be refrigerated in the appropriate one of his fleet of walk-in refrigerators.

He proudly shows the bottoms of sauté pans stowed beneath a counter. They look brand new but are almost thirty years old. Glassware appears to be aligned with the string of a surveyor. Roots, respect, and pride define this gentle and gifted man whose perfectionism is reflected in all aspects of his work.

"What makes a cuisine is the quality of your product and handling it gently with respect," he says. That is the key to his cooking and the reason he remains enamored of the cornucopia of vegetables grown in Rioja. Like a winemaker discussing vineyards, he rattles off the names of the farms near Berceo from which he buys his peppers and others in the Rioja Baja where he sources cauliflower. He does not see any difference between traditional cooking and modern cooking. What he sees is good cooking. He does not regard vegetables as a garnish or filler. To him, the proper cooking of vegetables is an essential part of gastronomy. This is why he treats the vegetables in his kitchen like children—only appropriate for the father of Riojan cuisine.

PEARS POACHED IN RIOJA

(PERAS DE RINCÓN DE SOTO AL VINO DE RIOJA)

Serves 6

Peras de Rincón are the succulent native species in Rioja, where there are groves of pear trees interspersed in the vineyards. Lorenzo Cañas poaches the pears in young Rioja wine with a touch of spice to balance the fruit of both the wine and pears.

Pairing: Semidulce White Rioja

---

1 bottle red Rioja Cosecha wine

1 cup granulated sugar

2 teaspoons black peppercorns

1 (3-inch) cinnamon stick

1 whole clove

6 firm but ripe pears, such as Bosc, about 5 ounces each

1. Combine the wine and sugar in a stainless steel or enameled saucepan. Tie the peppercorns, cinnamon stick, and clove in a square of cheesecloth or place the peppercorns and clove into a metal tea ball. Add the spices to the wine and bring the mixture to a boil over medium-high heat.

2. Peel the pears, leaving the stem attached. Core the pears through the bottom of the pear, using a small spoon or a melon baller.

3. Place the pears, standing upright, into the simmering wine. Reduce the heat to low and cook the pears, covered, for 20 to 25 minutes or until the pears are tender when pierced with the tip of a paring knife. Baste the pears during the cooking time. Remove the pears from the pan with a slotted spoon and place them in a mixing bowl.

4. Cook the poaching liquid over medium-high heat until reduced by one-half. Remove and discard the spices and pour the liquid over the pears. Cool to room temperature before serving, or serve chilled.

Note: The pears can be poached up to 2 days in advance and refrigerated, tightly covered.

MEAT-STUFFED PEPPERS

(PIMIENTOS RELLENOS DE CARNE)

Serves 6

Lorenzo Cañas makes this dish with the gloriously sweet *pimientos* that grow in Rioja. You may be able to find them at some farmers' markets during the summer, but the creamy meat filling is delicious in domestic peppers too.

Pairing: Alavesa Reserva (Subzonal)

---

12 (5- to 6-inch) piquillo peppers (Anaheim or poblano peppers can be substituted)

2 tablespoons unsalted butter

1 cup plus 2 tablespoons all-purpose flour

¾ cup whole milk

Salt and freshly ground black pepper

2 tablespoons olive oil

1 large onion, finely chopped

½ pound lean ground pork

½ pound lean ground beef

2 teaspoons paprika, preferably Spanish

3 large eggs

Vegetable oil for frying

1. Using a long-handled fork, char the peppers over the open flame of a gas stove or set a metal cooling rack over a burner on an electric stove and turn the peppers with tongs until the skin blackens on all sides. Place the peppers in a plastic bag and allow them to steam for 10 minutes. Remove the peppers from the bag and, when they are cool enough to handle, peel them, keeping them whole. Cut off the tops and remove the seeds. Set aside.

2. While the peppers cool, make the sauce. Melt the butter in a small saucepan over low heat. Stir in the 2 tablespoons of flour and cook, stirring constantly, for 2 minutes or until the mixture bubbles. Slowly but steadily pour the milk into the pan, whisking constantly over medium heat until the sauce comes to a boil. Simmer for 2 minutes, stirring constantly. Season to taste with salt and pepper, and set aside.

3. Heat the oil in a skillet over medium-high heat. Add the onion and cook, stirring frequently, for 3 to 5 minutes or until the onion is translucent. Crumble the pork and beef into the skillet and cook, breaking up lumps with a fork, for 5 to 7 minutes or until well browned. Add the paprika and season to taste with salt and pepper. Cook for 2 minutes. Stir in the sauce and cook for 1 minute. Allow the mixture to cool.

4. Gently stuff one-twelfth of the filling into each pepper through the hole in the top. Then refrigerate the peppers until cold, to facilitate frying.

5. Break the eggs in a shallow bowl and whisk well. Place the remaining 1 cup of flour on a plate. Pour 1½ inches of vegetable oil in a deep-sided skillet and heat the oil over medium-high heat to 375°F.

6. Dip the peppers into the flour, then into the egg, and then into the flour a second time. Place the coated peppers into the hot oil with tongs, being careful not to crowd the pan. Fry until brown and crisp on all sides, turning them gently with tongs. Remove the peppers from the oil with a slotted spatula and drain well on paper towels. Serve immediately.

Note: The peppers can be prepared up to the stage of coating and frying 1 day in advance and refrigerated, tightly covered with plastic wrap.

POTATOES WITH CHORIZO

(PATATAS RIOJANAS)

Serves 6

This is Lorenzo Cañas's version of a classic Riojan dish. He insists that a key to its success is to snap the potatoes to break them rather than dicing them neatly with a knife. Snapping causes the potatoes to release more starch into the broth, which thickens it.

Pairing: Modern Classic Crianza or Reserva

- ⅓ cup olive oil
- 1 large sweet onion, diced
- 1 green bell pepper, seeds and ribs removed, diced
- 1 small dried ancho chili, stemmed and broken into small pieces
- 2 teaspoons paprika, preferably Spanish
- 2 pounds Yukon gold potatoes
- 1 bay leaf
- ¾ pound chorizo in ¾-inch slices if thin or ¾-inch cubes if thick
- Salt and freshly ground black pepper

1. Heat the oil in a saucepan over medium-high heat. Add the onion, bell pepper, and chili and cook, stirring frequently, for 3 minutes or until the onion is translucent. Stir in the paprika and turn off the heat.

2. Peel the potatoes. Start a cut with a paring knife and then snap the potatoes into 2-inch chunks. Add the potatoes, bay leaf, and chorizo to the pan and add enough water to barely cover. Bring to a boil over medium-high heat, then cover the pan, reduce the heat to low, and simmer for 15 minutes or until the potatoes are tender.

3. Turn off the heat and allow the mixture to sit, covered, for 10 minutes to blend the flavors. Season to taste with salt and pepper, and serve immediately.

Note: The dish can be prepared up to 1 day in advance and refrigerated, tightly covered. Reheat it, covered, over low heat.

FRANCIS PANIEGO: FORGING A NEW FRONTIER FOR RIOJAN COOKING

When Pedro García and Andrea Echaurren looked at the future of their village of Ezcaray, set high in the Mountain Zone in the southwestern corner of La Rioja, they knew the arrival of the railroad in 1898 would make their commodious carriage house redundant, so they converted it to a hotel and began serving meals. Five generations later the Hotel Echaurren is still serving meals and has transitioned into the twenty-first century both in its sleek renovated space and in the cuisine served there by Francis Paniego, the chef at El Portal.

El Portal is the first restaurant in Rioja to receive a coveted star from the *Guide Michelin* in 2004 and has kept it ever since. Within the serene confines of a beige dining room with faux-stone trim, ten tables are arranged around windows overlooking a medieval church across the courtyard and beyond to the San Lorenzo Mountains, which are filled with skiers during winter months.

At the other end of the kitchen, Francis's mother, Marisa Sánchez, while slowing down, still oversees the preparation of updated Riojan classics such as potato croquettes and black pudding that are served at Echaurren Tradición, the restaurant for which she was honored as the Best Chef in Spain in 1987. That end of the kitchen features large cauldrons simmering on stoves; at Francis's end everything is *à la minute,* with touches of

molecular gastronomy and presentations as dramatic as a Dalí painting.

Francis credits his "immense luck" to Echaurren's loyal and seasoned clientele, who encouraged his provincial Riojan parents to expand his horizons and let him taste the world. His journey began when he finished high school at the Madrid Hospitality School.

In Madrid he lived with university students, many of whom trek today from all corners of the world to dine at El Portal in Ezcaray. But even with the sophistication of Madrid and the years that followed, he never lost the innocence and humility from his mountain village upbringing. His smile exudes genuine warmth, and his refreshing authenticity tends to hide his genius.

What Francis produces at El Portal is built on this solid Riojan base; you cannot improvise jazz until the classics have been mastered. But Francis's food is clearly bold and modern, tempered by his experiences in some of the most revered kitchens in Spain. He lists two apprenticeships working with Ferran Adrià, whom he calls "a total influence on my life," as the time his style truly evolved. His other mentors include two luminaries of Basque cuisine, Juan Mari Arzak and Pedro Subijana.

Before El Portal opened in 2003, when he was just thirty-five years old, some of Francis's modern dishes were appearing on the menu at his mother's restaurant.

The choice was then made to carry on the tradition of chefs in the family by forging his legacy.

It's not just dishes such as a tartare of tomato topped with a slowly roasted langoustine or squid served in a mayonnaise made from squid ink that have catapulted him to the top. It is also some of the small touches, such as a choice of seven olive oils from different regions of Spain and three salts that are served to diners along with a crisp wafer coated with pepitas and a thin olive stick.

Some of these touches are now also on the menu at the modern restaurant on the second level of the Marqués de Riscal Hotel. Francis consulted for the hotel, which opened in 2006 in Elciego in Rioja Alavesa, about a forty-minute drive from Ezcaray.

Francis's profile has been building internationally as he travels the world as an ambassador of Spanish cuisine. His passport is stamped with entries into the United States, Brazil, Sweden, England, France, Portugal, Belgium, and Italy. But Ezcaray is his love and his home. Marisa Sánchez and Félix Paniego, Francis's father, live in an apartment over El Portal. Francis and his wife and three children live about fifty yards away, as does his brother, José Félix, who is the sommelier for the two restaurants, and his family. There is little doubt that a sixth generation will someday take over this converted carriage barn.

ROASTED WHITE ASPARAGUS WITH MUSHROOM MAYONNAISE

(ESPÁRRAGOS NATURALES A LA PARRILLA CON MAYONESA DE PERRECHICOS)

Serves 4 to 6

White asparagus is a delectable spring treat in Rioja, and Francis prepares it as an appetizer with a mayonnaise made with fresh white mushrooms. The very low-temperature roasting of the asparagus makes it succulent and tender.

Pairing: Barrel-fermented white Rioja

- 1½ pounds thick fresh white asparagus
- 1 large egg yolk
- 1½ teaspoons freshly squeezed lemon juice
- 1 teaspoon white wine vinegar
- ¾ cup olive oil
- 3 ounces fresh white mushrooms, rinsed, trimmed, and finely chopped
- Salt and freshly ground white pepper
- 2 tablespoons finely snipped fresh chives

1. Preheat the oven to 175°F. Break off the woody ends from the asparagus and peel the bottom 2 inches. Arrange the asparagus in a shallow roasting pan and place in the oven for 4 hours. Set aside.

2. Place the egg yolk, lemon juice, and vinegar in a blender or food processor fitted with the steel blade. Puree until smooth. Add the olive oil 1 tablespoon at a time, allowing time between each addition. When all the oil is added and the mixture is very thick, add the mushrooms and puree until smooth. Season to taste with salt and pepper and refrigerate until ready to use.

3. To serve, place some asparagus on each plate and drizzle with the mayonnaise. Sprinkle with the chives and serve immediately.

Note: The asparagus can be roasted and the mayonnaise can be prepared up to 1 day in advance and refrigerated, tightly covered. Allow the asparagus to reach room temperature before serving.

CREAMY RICE WITH VEGETABLES AND TRUFFLES

(ARROZ MUY CREMOSO DE VERDURAS CON TRUFA)

Serves 6 to 8

This dish is very similar to an Italian risotto, but there is no sharp cheese to compete with the fabulously aromatic truffle. Fresh truffles are very expensive and are available only for a short time each fall, but truffle oil works just as well.

Pairing: Classic Rioja Reserva or Gran Reserva

- ¼ pound (1 stick) unsalted butter, divided
- 2 shallots, minced
- ½ pound fresh white mushrooms, trimmed and sliced
- 1 quart heavy cream
- Salt and freshly ground white pepper
- ½ medium onion, diced
- 1½ cups Arborio rice
- ¼ cup dry white wine
- 3 cups chicken stock, preferably homemade, heated to a simmer
- 1 small zucchini
- 1 fresh white truffle or 1 tablespoon white truffle oil

1. Heat 2 tablespoons of the butter in a skillet over medium-high heat. Add the shallots and cook, stirring frequently, for 2 minutes or until the shallots are translucent. Add the mushrooms and cook for an additional 5 minutes or until the mushrooms soften. Add the cream and bring to a boil. Reduce the heat to low and simmer the mixture until the cream is reduced by half. Season to taste with salt and pepper and set aside.

2. Heat the remaining butter in a saucepan over medium heat. Add the onion and cook, stirring frequently, for 2 minutes. Add the rice and cook for an additional 2 minutes, stirring to coat the grains with the butter. Add the wine and cook, stirring constantly, until it evaporates.

3. Add 1 cup of the stock and bring to a boil, stirring frequently. Reduce the heat to medium and simmer the rice, stirring frequently, for 5 minutes or until almost all the stock is absorbed. Add the remaining stock, cup by cup, in the same fashion.

4. Cut the zucchini in half and cut a ¼-inch thick slice of green skin lengthwise from one half. Finely chop the slice; reserve the remaining zucchini for another use.

5. Add the cream sauce and zucchini to the rice and cook for an additonal 5 minutes or until the rice is al dente. Season to taste with salt and pepper.

6. To serve, place a mound of rice on a plate and top with thinly sliced truffles or a drizzle of truffle oil. Serve immediately.

Note: The cream sauce can be prepared up to 2 days in advance and refrigerated, tightly covered. Heat it before adding it to the rice.

TOMATO TARTARE WITH LANGOUSTINE AND WHITE GARLIC

(TARTAR DE TOMATE CON CIGALA Y AJO BLANCO)

Serves 4

This variation on gazpacho deconstructs it so that the tomato is in the center and the creamy liquid spooned around it, flavored with garlic, is white. A fruity Rioja rosé would be excellent with this starter.

Pairing: Rioja Rosado

- 3 tablespoons olive oil
- 2 shallots, minced
- ¼ pound ripe plum tomatoes, cored, seeded, and finely chopped
- ⅛ pound dried dates, finely chopped
- ½ cup finely snipped fresh chives
- 1 teaspoon Worcestershire sauce
- Salt and freshly ground black pepper
- ⅓ pound whole blanched almonds
- 1 cup water
- 1 cup safflower oil or canola oil
- 2 garlic cloves, peeled
- 2 slices white bread, lightly toasted
- 2 tablespoons sherry vinegar
- 4 langoustines or large shrimp, cooked, peeled, and deveined, chilled

1. Heat the olive oil in a small skillet over medium heat. Add the shallots and cook, stirring frequently, for 3 minutes or until the shallots are translucent. Scrape the shallots into a mixing bowl.

2. Add the tomatoes, dates, chives, and Worcestershire sauce to the mixing bowl and season to taste with salt and pepper. Chill for 2 hours.

3. While the tomatoes chill, combine the almonds, water, oil, garlic, bread, and vinegar in a food processor fitted with the steel blade or in a blender. Puree until smooth and press the mixture through a sieve, pushing with the back of a spoon to extract as much liquid as possible. Discard the solids. Season the broth with salt and pepper, and chill.

4. To serve, pack ¼ of the tomato mixture into a ½-cup measure to mold it. Unmold in the center of a large shallow soup bowl and balance 1 shrimp on top of it. Serve the plates and then ladle ¼ of the almond broth around each of the tomato mounds.

Note: The almond broth can be prepared up to 2 days in advance and refrigerated, tightly covered.

BIBLIOGRAPHY

Amador de los Ríos, José. *Historia social, política y religiosa de los Judíos de España y Portugal,* Tomo II. Madrid, Spain: T. Fortanet, 1876.

Andrés Cabello, Sergio, and Carmen Bengoechea Escalona. *Descubrir la Sonsierra y Briones La Rioja.* Spain: Sepinum Publishing, 2008.

Araújo, Joaquín, and Daniel Acevedo. *LA RIOJA.* Museo Natural, Logroño, Spain: Daniel P. Acevedo, Images 2003.

Arte Vino magazine, no. 2, July 2009.

Ballesteros, Isolina. *Cine (ins)urgente.* Madrid, Spain: Edicional Fundamentos, 2001.

Banyols, Marie-Louise. "Rioja siempre renace." *Guía Peñín Sibaritas,* November 2008, 34.

Barco Royo, Emilio. *Análisis de un sector: El Rioja entre dos siglos.* Rioja, Spain: Gobierno de La Rioja, 2008.

Barco Royo, Emilio. *El Rioja entre dos siglos.* Cuaderno de Campo, Consejería de Agricultura del Gobierno de La Rioja, Logroño, Spain, August 2008.

Begg, Desmond. *Spain (Travellers Wine Guide).* New York: Sterling, 1990.

Brasch, Rabbi Rudolph. *Thank God I'm an Atheist.* Australia: Collins, 1987.

Burns, Tom. "Corridor of Power: The Thriving Economy That Has Sprung Up on the Banks of the River Ebro Is to Be Strengthened by Fresh Infrastructure." *Financial Times* [London], December 7, 1998, 1.

Candamo, Luis G., and Luis Vicente Elías. *Viña Tondonia: Un pago, una viña, un vino.* Logroño, Spain: Industrias Gráficas Castuera, 2007.

Cassidy, Chip. *Chip Cassidy's Wine Travels.* Coral Gables, FL: Crown Wine and Spirits, 2001.

Castro San Juan, Arachu. *Saber bien—Cultura y practicas alimentarias en la Rioja.* Logroño, Spain: Instituto de Estudios Riojanos, Gráficas Ochoa, S.A. 1998.

Contreras Villaseñor, Margarita, and Luís Vicente Elías Pastor. *Guía del turismo del vino.* Logroño, Spain: Editorial Piedra de Rayo, S.L., 2007.

Corsin, Maite, and José Peñín. "El retorno a los clásicos." *Guía Peñin Sibaritas*, November 2008, 6–14.

Croucher, Roland, et al. "The Jews and Alcohol." John Mark Ministries. January 7, 2009, http://jmm.aaa.net.au/articles/13487.htm.

De Mori, Lori. "Happy Trails." *Gourmet*, March 2009, 34–36.

Duijker, Hubrecht. *The Wines of Rioja.* London: Mitchell Beazley, 1985.

Egido Antonio. *La Estación Enológica de Haro.* Logroño, Spain: Ediciones La Prensa del Rioja, 2005.

Elías Pastor, Luis Vicente. *Guía de La Rioja.* Madrid, Spain: El País-Aguilar, 1992.

"El renacer del olivo en Rioja Alavesa." *Rioja Alavesa*, no. 3, Summer 2009, 38–43.

Facaros, Dana, and Michael Pauls. *Northern Spain*. London: Globe Pequot Press, 2001.

Fagan, Brian. *The Great Warming*. New York: Bloomsbury Press, 2008.

Fried, Eunice. *Burgundy: The Country, the Wines, the People*. New York: Harper & Row, 1986.

Fundación Camino de la Lengua Castellana, ed. *Camino de la lengua Castellana*. Logroño, Spain, 2000.

García Turza, Claudio. "Orñigenes del nombre Rioja y Español." Catedrático Universidad de La Rioja: Spain. Personal interview, October 1, 2010.

Gobierno de La Rioja, ed. *Guía completa de los vinos de La Rioja*. Logroño, Spain, 2004.

Gobierno de La Rioja. Consejería Agricultura y Desarrollo Económico. III Foro Mundial del Vino: Rioja III Milenio. Editorial Gráficas Cícero, S.L., 2004.

Gobierno de La Rioja, ed. *La Rioja paisajes del vino*. Logroño, Spain, 2008.

Gobierno de La Rioja, ed. *La Rioja—Sus viñas y su vino*. Logroño, Spain, 2009.

Gómez González, Eduardo. *Cocina Riojana*. León, Spain: Editorial Everest S.A., 2005.

Gómez Urdáñez, José Luis. *El Rioja histórico, la denominación de origen y su consejo regulador*. Logroño, Spain: IMSA, S.A., 2000.

González Ochoa, José María. *Riojanos pioneros en Indias*. Estella, Navarre, Spain: Gráficas Lizarra, 2006.

"Guide of the Best Fruits and Vegetables—La Rioja." June 26, 2009, http://www.frutas-hortalizas.com/pdf_UK09/128_137.pdf.

Hamilton, Thomas J. *Appeasement's Child*. New York: Knopf, 1943.

Hemingway, Ernest. *For Whom the Bell Tolls*. New York: Scribner, 1940.

Herbermann, Charles George, and Knights of Columbus Catholic Truth Committee. *The Catholic Encyclopedia: An International Work of Reference on the Constitution, Doctrine, Discipline, and History of the Catholic Church*. Cambridge, MA: Encyclopedia Press, 1913, 187–188, http://books.google.com/books?id=QeSrDhhXPf8C.

Huetz de Lemps, Alain. *La agitada historia de los vinos de España en el campo*. Bilbao, Spain: Servicio de Estudios del Banco Bilbao: Vizcaya, no. 130, 1994.

Huetz de Lemps, Alain. "La lucha tenaz de Don Manuel Quintano en favor de la calidad de los vinos Riojanos (1787–1806)." *Berceo*, 1995, no. 129, 169–174.

Ibáñez, Santiago, and Jesús Saez Monge. *Cocina y monasterios en La Rioja: El vino y los 5 sentidos*. Logroño, Spain: Gobierno de La Rioja, 2001.

Ibáñez Rodríguez, Miguel. "Vine and Vineyards in Medieval Rioja." University of Valladolid, Spain. Personal interview, September 4, 2009.

International Society of Mushroom Science. "The Cultivation of Mushroom in the South East Region of Spain 'La Manchuela,'" http://www.isms.biz/article10.htm.

Jefford, Andrew. *The New France.* London, Great Britain: Mitchell Beazley, 2002.

Johnson, Hugh. *Vintage: The Story of Wine.* New York: Simon & Schuster, 1989.

Kramer, Matt. "What It Really Takes." *Wine Spectator,* August 31, 2008.

"La DOP Peras de Rincón de Soto renueva su imagen y patrocinará la vuelta ciclista a España." *La Rioja Calidad,* http://www.lariojacalidad.org/.

Larreina Díaz, Mikel, and Luis Planet. *Vinos y bodegas de Rioja.* Barcelona, Spain: Luís Tolosa Planet and LT&A Ediciones, 2005

Larreina Díaz, Mikel, and Miguel Ángel Larreina González. *Rioja Alavesa: El gran vino del País Vasco.* Vitoria-Gasteiz, Spain: Imprenta de la Diputación Foral de Àlava, 2006.

La Rioja: Art Treasures and Wine-Growing Resources. Barcelona, Spain: Editorial Escudo de Oro, S.A., 1981.

Llano Gorostiza, M. "Los vinos de Rioja." Bilbao *Induban,* 1974.

Macías Kapón, Uriel, and Elena Romero. *Los Judíos de Europa.* Madrid, Spain: Alianza Editorial, 2005.

Manguel, Alberto. "Rioja: Taste of History." *Food and Wine,* October 2002.

Marín, Diego. *La civilización Española.* New York: Holt, Rinehart and Winston, 1969.

Marino Pascual, Jesús. *Museo de la Cultura del Vino Dinastía Vivanco arquitectura.* Museo de la Cultura del Vino Dinastía Vivanco, Bilbao, Spain: Mccgraphics Planta Elkar, 2005.

Martín Rodríguez, José Luis. *El vino y la buena mesa medieval.* Logroño, Spain: UNED Rioja, 1998.

Marquina, Don Pedro. *Un Cosechero Riojano.* Teatro Salon Eslava, Madrid Plaza de los Carros, December 1871.

Martínez Tomé, Atilano. *El monasterio Cisterciense en el origen de los vinos españoles.* Madrid, Spain: Ministerio de Agricultura, Pesca y Alimentación, 1991.

Miller, Townsend. *The Castles and the Crown: Spain 1451–1555,* London: Lowe and Brydone, 1963.

Muro Munilla, Miguel Ángel. *El cáliz de letras: Historia del vino en la literatura.* Logroño, Spain: Reproziur, S.A. (Logroño: Fundación Dinastía Vivanco para la Investigación y Divulgación de la Cultura e Historia del Vino), 2006.

Olcoz Yanguas, Serafín. *Fitero Cisterciense del Monasterio a la Villa (Siglos XII–XV).* Tudela, Tracasa, M.I. Ayuntamiento de Fitero, 2008.

Paniego, Francis, and Marisa Sánchez. *Echaurren.* Barcelona, Spain: Montagud Editores, S.A., 2008.

Pascual Corral, Javier. *El vino de Rioja.* Logroño, Spain: La Prensa del Rioja, 2003.

Peñín, José. *12 Great Spanish Bodegas.* Madrid, Spain: PI&Erre Ediciones, 1996.

Peñín, José, Carlos González, Maite Corsin, and Federico Oldenburg. *Peñín Guide to Spanish Wine 2008,* 18th ed. Madrid, Spain: Grupo Peñin, 2008.

Preston, Paul. *Las tres Españas del 36.* Barcelona, Spain: Plaza & Janés Editores, 1998.

Prial, Frank J. "Wine Talk." *New York Times,* October 12, 1988, C12.

Radford, John. *The Wines of Rioja.* London: Octopus, 2004.

Ramírez Pascual, Tomás. *La Rioja donde se encontraba y que significa.* Logroño, Spain: BELEZOS Instituto de Estudios Riojanos, June 2009.

Richardson, Paul. *A Late Dinner.* New York: Simon & Schuster, 2007.

Romero, Elena, and Uriel Macías. *Los Judíos de Europa.* Alianza Editorial, 2005.

Roth, Norman. *Medieval Jewish Civilization: An Encyclopedia,* Vol. 12. UK: Routlege, 2009.

Scarborough, Ron. *Rioja and Its Wines.* London: Survival Books, 2000.

"Seder-Bound? What to Pour." *The Nibble,* January 7, 2009, http://www.thenibble.com/reviews/main/wine/kosher-for-passover-wines.asp.

Thomas, Hugh. *La guerra civil española,* Vols. I and II. Barcelona, Spain: Grijalbo Mondadori, S.A. 1976.

Unwin, Tim. *El vino y la viña.* Barcelona, Spain: Tusquets Editor, 2002.

Weaver Dorning, Amy. "Ultimate Access the Wine Cellar." *Town and Country,* November 2008.

White, David. "A Measure of Quantity with Quality." *Financial Times* [London], December 7, 1998, 3.

ACKNOWLEDGMENTS

Regardless of nationality, most serious writers realize that it is their immediate families who make the biggest sacrifices for them to complete their projects. In that vein, I must thank my four children, who patiently and with natural understanding and love stood by me as I stole hours and entire days from them. Sunday morning breakfasts, weekends, evenings—all disappeared as I became saturated in Rioja. My children have fueled me in so very many ways, and they are all heroes in their own right: Anthony for your self-motivation and being my right-hand man throughout the years; Nick for your original thought, pure heart, and ability to think outside the box; Harrison, my gentle giant, for your sense of calm and the security that has always brought me comfort and joy; and Adriana, my heroine, who at fifteen kilos taught me what courage and strength felt like on a daily basis. You gifted me with stamina and power beyond what I ever thought I was capable of. To all four of you, I extend equal thanks.

To Kevin Zraly, father of my children, my partner in life's greatest joys and most painful suffering, and the ultimate wine educator. We are six souls that have journeyed deep. I probably don't say it enough, but I love you all more than words can say.

Also, I must acknowledge my parents, Anthony and Marie Fabiano, who instilled in me the importance of education and fueled a passion for continual learning that defies gravity. Their World War II spirit of self responsibility, resiliency, loyalty, and hard work defines me. Additionally, my sister, Laurie Fabiano, who has rescued me one too many times and has always been there for me. My brother Anthony and my sister-in-law Carole give me their love and encouragement, and my brother-in-law Joe fed me as I pursued the depths of Rioja.

To Ellen Brown, my first-class editor of consummate professionalism, who organized my Riojan world, my gratitude is as deep as the research for this book. For centuries the practice of transmitting knowledge through grand masters and mentorship was critical at the Yuso monastery of Rioja. In that tradition, I extend enormous gratitude to José Luis Lapuente, Emilio Barco, and Javier Pascual, who were mentors beyond measure and are referenced in the bibliography.

Thank you to the La Rioja government, which gave me its trust and support to be a voice for the region. To the Rioja Regulatory Control Board and the Enological Station of Haro; both provide the framework and platform from which a region can grow in diversity, quality, and solidarity. I believe in all of you as much as you believe in me.

The public relations director of the Tourist Office of Spain, Pilar Vico, deserves special thanks. In 2001, I approached her to write a book and she put her faith in me. The devastation of September 11 prohibited that project but ultimately birthed this book.

The Dinastía Vivanco family made me feel welcome as I worked in their documentation center for countless hours cloaked in quintessential Riojan hospitality. Librarian Nuria del Río helped me access information and served as a human dictionary, defining ancient concepts and interpreting old Castilian. To the Vibrant Rioja team that works with daily talent and tenacity to bring the best of Rioja to all corners of the United States.

I would also like to acknowledge for their support and encourgement: Pedro Sanz, Alonso, Víctor Pascual Artacho, Îñigo Nagore, Pedro Sáez, Igor Fonseca, Juan Bautista, Ricardo Aguiriano, Rebeca Gómez, Estíbaliz Aguado, and Katherine Camargo.

Professional friends with similar Spanish-American paths, Paul Vella and Janet Kafka, thank you for standing at my side for this past decade. And Miguel Ibáñez, expert in the vines of the Middle Ages, who effortlessly connected two critical centuries for me, I thank you and Pablo as well as the Tourist Office of Rioja.

Special thanks to the entire Sterling team under the leadership of Marcus Leaver, Jason Prince, and my enthusiastic and wise editorial director Carlo DeVito as well as Diane Abrams and Brita Vallens. The "Sterling Standards" were clear from the onset.

Finally, I would like to thank many friends and colleagues in Rioja as well as every single Riojan I met as I traveled and studied their *tierra*. Their eagerness to help and share the intricacies of their homeland was inspiring and infectious. This work is possible due to all of you and I extend to you my blessings and gratitude.

INDEX

Note: Page numbers in *italics* include photographs or illustrations
(including wine labels). Page numbers in **bold** indicate recipes.

PICTURE CREDITS

Daniel Acevedo: ii-iii, vi, viii, 5, 11, 12, 15, 16, 19, 20, 23, 27, 29, 32, 35, 36, 48, 52, 53 (bottom), 55, 59, 63, 68, 71, 72, 81, 86, 88-89, 95, 98, 99, 100-101, 103, 126-127, 177, 180-181, 213 (top and bottom), 227, 229, 242

Rafael Lafuente: 7, 39 (top left and bottom), 44, 134, 140-141.

Juan Carlos Marijuán: 33, 34, 50-51, 53 (top), 57, 60, 61, 62

Marina Donezar Pérez: 42, 43

Miguel Ángel Robredo: i, xii-xiii, xiv-1, 2, 3 (bottom), 25, 31, 46-47, 65, 66-67, 69 (top and bottom), 78, 83, 108-109, 110, 111 (bottom), 128

Individual wineries graciously provided photographs of their property, equipment, and labels. Exceptions are listed below.

v: Image courtesy the Enological Station of Haro

3 (top): Rioja Council of Agriculture

37: Fernando Díaz

39: Ingrid Fernández (top right)

48: Sergio Aja

49: BEA Olive Oil Image courtesy of Paul Vella, Ken Krimstein, and RIHUELO S.L.

75: courtesy of Dinastía Vivanco

77: courtesy of Mr. Javier Pascual/La Prensa del Rioja

90: courtesy of Vineyard Brands, Inc. and Bodegas Marqués de Cáceres.

111 (top), 112: courtesy of Dinastía Vivanco

116: photo © Underdog Wine Merchants, Livermore, CA

121: Rioja Council of Agriculture

129: Bodegas Y Viñedos Labastida (bottom); courtesy of the Enological Station of Haro (top)

130: courtesy of Riojawine.com/The Regulatory Board of the Denominación de Origen Calificada Rioja

133: photo by Jose María Muguruza, courtesy of Jesús Madrazo

135: photo by Jesús R. Rocandio, courtesy of La Rioja Alta, S.A.

143: Campo Viejo, courtesy of Pernod Ricard USA

145: Courtesy of José Luis Lapuente, Secretary General, D.O.Ca Rioja, Rioja Regulatory Control Board

148, 149: Courtesy of R. López de Heredia Viña Tondonia, S.A./Pepe Franco

150–151: Courtesy of the Enological Station of Haro

158: Campo Viejo, courtesy of Pernod Ricard USA

166: Courtesy of R. López de Heredia/Viña Tondonia

167: courtesy of Maison Marques & Domaines/Marques de Murrieta

176: Bodegas Valdemar

178/179: Ysios, courtesy of Domecq Bodegas

184: Bodegas Baigorri, courtesy of DFV Wines

185: courtesy of La Rioja Alta, S.A.

186: Barón De Ley, courtesy of Frederick Wildman & Sons (left); Bodegas Beronia courtesy of González Byass (right)

187: Bodegas Bretón courtesy of Classical Wines

188: Property of Bodegas Darien

189: Bodegas El Coto, courtesy of Frederick Wildman & Sons

190: Heredad Ugarte, S.A. (left), Bodegas Lan S.A., courtesy of Monsieur Touton

191: Bodegas Marqués de Cáceres, courtesy of Vineyard Brands

193: © Fernando Díaz (right)

198: Courtesy of Grupo Familia Martínez Bujanda/Bodega Finca Valpiedra

199: Bodegas Valsacro/Kysela Pere et Fils, Ltd.

200: Bodegas Y Viñedos Labastida/Winebow, Inc.

202/203: Ysios, courtesy of Domecq Bodegas

204: Bodegas Ostatu S.L. (left); Pagos del Rey S.L., courtesy of Félix Solís Avantis (right)

205: Bodegas Montebuena, courtesy of Kysela Pere et Fils, Ltd.

207: Marqués de Tomares, S.L., courtesy of Parador Selections, LLC

208: Compañía Bodeguera de Valenciso, courtesy of Classical Wines (top left)

210/211, 217, 221: Courtesy of Lorenzo Cañas

212: Sergio Aja

223: Courtesy of Francis Paniego